MOVING UP
TO MANAGEMENT

MOVING UP TO MANAGEMENT

Nick Thornely and Dan Lees

A practical guide from basics to boardroom

ARROW
BUSINESS BOOKS

Published by Arrow Books in 1994

1 3 5 7 9 10 8 6 4 2

Arrow Books Limited
20 Vauxhall Bridge Road, London SW1V 2SA

Random House Australia (Pty) Limited
20 Alfred Street, Milsons Point, Sydney,
New South Wales 2061, Australia

Random House New Zealand Limited
18 Poland Road, Glenfield,
Auckland 10, New Zealand

Random House South Africa (Pty) Limited
PO Box 337, Bergvlei, South Africa

Random House UK Limited Reg. No. 954009

ISBN 0 09 941521 6

Phototypeset by Intype, London

Printed and bound in Great Britain by
The Guernsey Press Co. Ltd., Vale, Guernsey.

Contents

PART ONE

Taking Over

ONE

Moving Up

Moving up to management is one of the most important moves you will ever make because, as a manager, you are a member of a group whose decisions and actions affect all of us, influencing our working lives, our entertainment, the products we buy and ultimately the quality of the air we breathe.

In the workplace this influence is direct and obvious because managers are in the people business and, as a new manager, instead of just doing the work allotted to you, you will find yourself working through other people.

Put like that, the job of management sounds simple, but in fact getting other people to do as you wish is far from easy, while some managers never master the art of allowing others to do things they think they themselves could do better.

LEADERS AND FOLLOWERS

In moving up to management you have become a *leader* rather than a follower, which means that as well as mastering the nuts and bolts of *administration* you must be able to:

- *motivate* people to do what you want them to do;
- *delegate*, which means not only giving people a task but also allowing them everything they need – including the authority – to carry it out.

As a new manager you are in the front line, working in direct and daily contact with the rank and file. It is your character and abilities which will shape the working lives of every member of your staff and help them to become happy and efficient members of a smoothly functioning team.

In addition to this you have to act as a conduit, transmitting information both vertically between the rank and file and your superiors and horizontally between yourself and other managers on the same grade.

This makes you a person of vital importance, both to your team and to your organization as a whole, which means that the first promotion to management is a crucial one.

This has not always been recognized, but the management revolution, which began some 50 years ago, is now in full swing, and as a new manager you will be in a position to enjoy all the benefits and bear all the responsibilities of the new-style management.

THE MANAGEMENT REVOLUTION

For many new managers who are, almost by definition, youthful, it is sometimes difficult to remember that the 'dark Satanic mills' of the Industrial Revolution really existed – and persisted – and that they were run mainly by people who thought that the only way they could get employees to work was to threaten them with the sack or to bribe them with a few pence more in wages.

Paradoxically, it was the need to educate the workers to the point where they could operate the new machines which changed the character of the workforce. Workers who were taught to read and write developed a thirst for education and began to want more from life than a bare existence. Slowly, employers began to realize that by managing the 'new' workforce in the old way they were wasting one of their most valuable resources, and that what they needed to do was to harness the ideas and enthusiasm of the people who worked for them. A new sort of management – and a new sort of manager – were needed to manage the new workforce.

SMILE! YOUR NEW JOB'S BEEN UPGRADED

The managerial revolution has led to the virtual disappearance of the old-fashioned, sergeant-major-type supervisor whose main function was to maintain discipline and ensure that the orders of middle management were carried out. The 'superior' work-force of today needs a superior type of management and, as a result, the job of the front-line manager has been upgraded.

Today, managers – and especially front-line managers – are increasingly required to motivate their subordinates, to train them and help them to produce better results, while allowing them to manage a great deal of their own work. In effect, as the rank and file assume some of the responsibilities once exercised by front-line managers, the front-line managers themselves are exercising some of the functions that were once the prerogative of middle management.

ENTER THE TEAM COACH

This means that, as a new manager, you will be required to act, not as a workplace 'policeman' and disciplinarian, but as a team coach responsible for training and morale as well as your team's performance. In fact, in order to make the change in emphasis obvious to everyone, some large companies now refer to their managers as 'team coaches' and their chief executive officer as the 'head coach'.

This change to 'teams' and team coaching has made things more satisfying and agreeable for all concerned and, as 'team' derives from a word meaning 'family', the choice of name is particularly happy. However, while the image of the manager as a coach, encouraging and guiding his workplace 'family', is one which well expresses the new attitude to management, it is worth bearing in mind that:

- sports team coaches are not normally 'soft', nor are they people who have abandoned their authority; ask any top athlete. They are usually extremely competent individuals, often ex-athletes themselves, who know how to motivate their teams to give their best and *to win*;
- in most progressive organizations, managers (and especially front-line managers) have become 'team coaches' rather than bullying sergeant-majors, does not imply that the objectives of management have changed, but only that

the methods have become more sophisticated, more people-friendly and – more effective.

WHAT DO MANAGERS DO?

Even though most employees now know more about what managers do than ever before, you might still get some funny answers if you were to ask the people who work on the shop floor or in offices, 'What do managers do?'

In fact, the function of managers is to ensure the optimal use of the resources available to them, both material and human, in order to further the aims of the organization which employs them.

Managers can be divided into three main groups: senior managers who lay down policy and create strategies; middle managers who develop and implement strategies; and front-line managers who plan and implement tactics. The activities of all three grades are directed towards the achievement of the organization's aims.

In order to make these aims clear to their employees of all grades, many organizations now publish a form of 'mission statement', which may include such laudable aims as job satisfaction and security for employees, respect for the environment and participation in the life of the local community. However, it is worth remembering that organizations which are inefficient wither away and companies which fail to make a profit go out of business. In both cases they are powerless to carry out any of their objectives, however worthwhile.

Managers are using the humanistic methods we shall be discussing in this book *because they work*.

VICTOR VROOM AND THE NEW MANAGER

The superbly named American motivation psychologist Victor Vroom asserts that there are three questions people ask when taking on a job. They are questions that are particularly pertinent in the case of people who are moving up to management. According to Vroom you should ask yourself:

- will I be able to do what I am being asked to do?
- what are the rewards on offer?
- would I want the rewards on offer?

WILL YOU BE ABLE TO DO THE JOB?

Even when they have proved their worth in the office or on the shop floor, many people are apprehensive when faced with their first promotion, even though they may have worked hard to earn it. To them, moving up to management is a journey into uncharted territory with potentially hostile inhabitants whose language and customs are a mystery. Worse still, it appears to be an area in which their experience to date will count for little and where almost everything has to be relearned.

In fact, although the move up to management is an important career watershed which entails acquiring new skills and developing others, it is by no means the leap in the dark it may appear. This is because almost all of us, even while still members of the rank and file, have had considerable experience of 'management', both in the workplace and outside it.

Moving up to management involves becoming a full-time 'professional' with all that the word implies in the shape of training, dedication and responsibility. However, like an amateur footballer who joins the professional ranks, you will at least have some experience to assist you in making the change.

WE ARE ALL MANAGERS

As an adult you will already have had experience of looking after and obtaining the best from your most valuable resource – *yourself*. If you are married, and especially if you have a family, you may well have had experience of managing a team and will certainly have had to learn how to manage finite material resources.

In the workplace, as a member of the rank and file, whatever your job, you will already have had to make some 'managerial' decisions and, as the tendency is increasingly towards empowerment, you may have been in charge of a great deal of your particular process.

The following checklist will give you some idea of how you have been 'managing' even before moving up to management.

HOW HAVE YOU 'MANAGED' SO FAR?

- Do you keep physically fit and mentally alert?
- Are you usually appropriately dressed and smartly turned out?
- Has life made you self-confident, well-balanced and resilient?
- Are you reasonably well-read and well-informed?
- Are you punctual?
- Do you make lists, establish personal schedules and stick to them, or keep a diary?
- Are you able to think 'laterally'?
- What is your attitude to worries? Are you able to examine them honestly and turn them into problems capable of solution, or do you just leave them and hope they will go away?
- Can you usually manage on your current income or do you almost always find that you have 'too much month left at the end of the money'?
- Are you able to work out a detailed budget and stick to it?
- Do you take good care of your material possessions and budget for their eventual replacement where necessary?
- Do you make shopping lists and plan meals in advance?
- Can you cope with crisis? Do you know where to find expert help when needed e.g. a doctor or a plumber?
- If you have a family, do you consult your partner or your family before making decisions which concern them?
- Have you any experience of organizing sports teams, charity events, etc.?
- If you have held any official position with teams, clubs and so on, how did you cope with committee work? Were you able to handle dissent?
- Does much of your work involve making decisions?
- Have you ever been asked to stand in for your boss?

- Do your colleagues tend to look to you for guidance when there is a crisis?
- Do you usually find that you are able to persuade other people to do what you wish them to do?

WHAT SORT OF MANAGER WILL YOU MAKE?

The chances are that you have been doing a lot more managing than you thought and that your 'amateur' experience of management will stand you in good stead as a professional manager.

If you are able to give a positive answer to most of the questions on the checklist, you have been 'managing' well so far and have a sound basis of experience on which to build.

SOMEBODY UP THERE LIKES YOU

If you still have any lingering doubts about your ability to fill the position of front-line manager, remind yourself that you were almost certainly given the job because one or more knowledge-able and experienced persons were convinced that you could do it and do it well. In many cases they will have risked their reputations on their estimate of your character and abilities.

In addition to your experience and the endorsement of your employers, the fact that you are reading this book indicates that you intend to do your best and that you are willing to learn. You need have no worries as to your ability to do the job.

Remind yourself of this from time to time as confidence is one of the most effective weapons in the managerial armoury.

WHAT ARE THE REWARDS?

The second of Vroom's questions asks: 'If I can do the job, what rewards are on offer?'. In the case of moving up to management you could expect the rewards to include:

- *more money.* Still one of the most important rewards in respect of both its intrinsic value and as a success 'marker';
- *improved status.* You are the 'manager', the 'skipper', the

'boss' with a clipboard or your name on a door to show the world you are 'somebody';

- *esteem.* Your efforts have been recognized and now that you have a higher profile there is a good chance that they will be appreciated at their full value;
- *responsibility.* You will now be responsible for your own performance and for the performance of your team. This will help you to realize your full potential;
- *a career.* By contrast with people in many other professions – for example, doctors who, unless they specialize, remain in general practice from 27 to 65 – as a new manager you are beginning a career which could lead to your running a company or even an organization the size of a small country.

WILL YOU ENJOY BEING A MANAGER?

Vroom's third question asks: 'Will I like the rewards on offer?' and as a new manager you will almost certainly have decided that the answer is 'Yes'.

Money is usually particularly important for younger people, while almost everyone appreciates increased status and the esteem of others. You will also enjoy the feeling of maturity that comes with the knowledge that you are responsible for other people as well as for yourself.

However, perhaps the thing you will enjoy most about being a new manager is the feeling that you are on the move and that, in these days of virtual meritocracy, the sky really could be the limit.

SUMMARY

- Why your job as a new manager is important to you, to your people and to your organization.
- Why you need to be able to motivate, to administer and to delegate.
- The Management Revolution. Why more sophisticated employees need more sophisticated management and how

this has led to the upgrading of your job as a front-line manager.

- The change from the front-line manager as a workplace 'policeman' to the front-line manager as a 'team coach', and why this does not mean that management has gone 'soft'.
- Why you can be confident about your ability to do your new job. A 'management' experience check-list.
- Why you will enjoy the rewards of moving up to management which include not only more money and improved status but also – unlike many other professions – a potential field marshal's baton in your desk drawer.

TWO

Moving In

Right! You've got the promotion. The move up to management is yours and has been duly celebrated with congratulations from your friends and family, a party and couple of private choruses of *Tannenbaum* to remind you that you really have 'got the boss's job at last'.

However, the euphoria engendered by your promotion can begin to fade as the morning approaches when you have to report either to a new workplace run by complete strangers, or your old workplace staffed by people who, perhaps for some years, have been your colleagues and friends.

In either case you should be officially presented to your staff by your immediate superior as this helps to validate your authority. If there is no suggestion from your superior that this should be done, bring up the matter yourself as, if your subordinates find a stranger in the boss's chair when they report for work, it could get your first management job off to a bad start.

New managers who move up in their old department face a different set of problems from those encountered by those who take over a different department in the same organization, or move to a new company. Because of this, many companies arrange for new managers who are going to take charge of their old department to go on a course, or at least to take a few days' holiday before starting their new job.

Whether your staff are familiar faces or new faces, the day you move in as the manager is an important one and it makes sense to prepare for it.

A NEW JOB – A NEW ROLE

Moving up to management will give you one of the best chances you will ever have to modify the way you are perceived by other people – by adapting to the new part you have to play. If you are moving to a new organization or a new department your subordinates will not have seen you in your old role as one of the rank and file, and if you are taking over your old department your ex-colleagues will be expecting you to change with your new role.

This means that before you take over you should give some thought to your new role and how you intend to fill it. Normally you will not have to make any drastic changes but you could decide, for example, that a more mature attitude is called for now that you are no longer a carefree member of the rank and file.

THE CIA RULE

Don't worry. This CIA has nothing to do with cloak and dagger operations. It's just a handy mnemonic to help you get your priorities straight and, while its application is general, the rule is particularly applicable to front-line management.

The initials stand for *C-ontrol*, *I-nfluence* and *A-cademic* and, outside the workplace, you could expect for example to *control* much of your personal spending and to *influence* the way in which your local authority spends its money. On the other hand, whereas any effect you can have on the government's fiscal policy is largely *academic*, your effect on, say, the weather is totally so, even though you will be interested in both.

The CIA Rule has many specific applications; for example, as a stress-avoidance mechanism when dealing with problems or crises – which we shall be looking at later. We shall also be applying it to the whole of this book by concentrating on those factors of your job as a new manager which you may reasonably expect to control or influence, while providing a certain amount of information about those areas in which your influence is liable to be academic.

Modifying your appearance and character is a good example of an area in which you can exercise control. Fortunately there are many areas which front-line managers *can* control, the importance of which is not diminished by the fact that they usually involve little or no expenditure and do not need the authorization or agreement of others.

THE MANAGER'S JOKE SYNDROME

Some modification of your character and appearance may be needed because of the manager's joke syndrome.

Few established managers have any idea what an important part 'manager watching' plays in the lives of the staff, but as a new manager you will still be aware of this. You will have noticed, for example, that the manager's jokes always get a good laugh from the staff, a tacit admission of the position managers hold in the eyes of those around them.

Even thinking aloud can be hazardous. Remember King Henry II who mused, 'Who will free me from this turbulent priest?' and later discovered that two of his knights had taken his words seriously and had murdered Archbishop Becket in his own cathedral.

Don't forget that from now on everything you say or do in the workplace will have at least double the effect – good or bad – that it did when you were a member of the rank and file. Managers are always 'on parade'.

Points you might consider before taking over include:

- *dress*. This depends on the workplace but any suit should be of good quality and leaning towards the conservative.
  Women could try a little power dressing with, for example, a tailored suit relieved by one very feminine luxury item.
  You can always change to a more flamboyant style once you have settled in;
- *manners*. Usually your approach will be slightly more formal than it was, but make courtesy your rule. Bear in mind the old joke about being nice to people on your way up in case you meet them again on your way down.

One decision you may have to make is whether you want to
be on first name terms with your staff, an especially difficult
choice if they have been calling you by your first name, or
your nickname, for years;

- *attitude*. Think about what sort of boss you would like to be.
Obviously your attitude will be governed to some extent by
the sort of people who make up your team, but 'Manage as
you would be managed by' is a good rule of thumb,
especially if you have a role model in the form of a boss you
have worked for.

MANAGING FRIENDS

Having to manage one's friends is not normally a problem if
you are taking over a completely strange department as your
socializing with your staff will usually be with groups rather than
individuals.

Taking over a department in which you have worked is different and many new managers worry about having to give orders
to their friends and perhaps even one day having to fire them.
In fact, the situation is rarely as difficult as new managers imagine
it will be.

This is because:

- your friends, along with the rest of your former colleagues,
will tend to respect the 'psychological contract' which requires
them to regard you as their hierarchic superior;
- in your new role you may already have begun to distance
yourself from your former colleagues by slightly more
formal behaviour;
- the problem will almost certainly begin to solve itself as you
make friends with other managers of the same status whose
problems and interests you share.

In the case of a friend who has become close to you, and perhaps
to your family, to the extent that you are virtually inseparable
outside the workplace, you could have a problem, not so much
with your friend, but with the other members of your depart-

15

ment. In some cases it might be best to arrange for your friend's transfer to another department.

GUNS BLAZING OR 'SOFTLY SOFTLY'?

Some management theorists believe with Machiavelli that when you take over a new job as manager, at whatever level, you should go in with guns blazing and make any unpopular changes you have to make immediately.

This may be the case if you are taking over as manager of a department in which you have already worked and have been planning your first moves for some time but, if you adopt a town-taming attitude in an unfamiliar workplace, you could easily get rid of a few of the goodies by mistake. In fact it's usually best to spend some time getting to know people by listening to what everyone has to say and making a careful study of your predecessor's files. Use any information you acquire in this way as background only. It is up to you to make your own assessment of both your human and material resources.

WHAT DID THE LAST MANAGER DIE OF?

It's useful to know how your predecessor went about the job of managing and how successful they were from the point of view of their team and of their superiors.

Why did they leave? Have they retired, been promoted, or left the company? If they have left, did they fall or were they pushed?

TAKING OVER FROM SUPERMAN OR WONDERWOMAN

If you are taking over a department in which you have already worked, from a manager you are happy to treat as a role model, you can afford to take your time and to build on his or her success. You may even be able to call on them for a little behind-the-scenes help while you are finding your feet.

You may run into some 'Mrs Jones always did things this way' comments from both your staff and your superiors but this sort of nostalgia rarely lasts very long. In fact, the only real problem in taking over from a highly successful and popular manager is that you may have to work hard to make your own successes apparent.

TAKING OVER FROM A FAILURE

Taking over from someone who has not succeeded, or was unpopular either with staff or higher management, could provide you with a real chance to shine, unless of course your predecessor was fighting a losing battle against problems like inefficient staff or lack of senior management support.

It is up to you to decide whether you have inherited your predecessor's worries or merely the results of their failure to cope with the everyday problems of management. Either way, anything you do is almost bound to be an improvement and you will be given credit for any success.

However, an unsuccessful predecessor could have left you some major worries in the shape of a bitter and resentful workforce, in which case your problem will be to gain their trust before you can persuade them that you intend changing things for the better.

TURNING THE RUNNER-UP INTO YOUR NUMBER TWO

If your new team includes someone who was an unsuccessful candidate for your job, you could find yourself testing your people skills on a person who is convinced that they should be sitting in your chair. They may even have persuaded themselves that they were 'promised the job', in which case they will see you as a usurper. This is one problem which will get worse if it is not dealt with immediately and a good way to tackle it might be to enlist the aid of the person concerned.

Invite them to come and see you for a private talk and, after a couple of minutes' chat, lay things on the line: 'I know you were in the running for this job, Mike, and I can understand how you feel. However, the fact that you were a candidate means that you are considered management material. My position is that, in order to make ours a successful team, I am going to need someone who is "thinking management" and who has already given some thought to how the department should be organized. If you would like to help me to plan and improve the team's performance, it would be good experience for you as well as being useful exposure. What do you say we give it a try?'

In just a few minutes, without committing yourself on a long-term basis, you will have defused a potentially awkward, if not dangerous, situation, asked for help, which is often a good move, and suggested to the person concerned how *they* might benefit from helping you. You may even have recruited a keen and efficient deputy.

MEETING YOUR TEAM

You should already have been introduced to your staff as a group and you now need to arrange individual meetings for every member of the team. Try to get as much information about the person concerned as possible before the interview and use the first couple of minutes to flesh out this knowledge.

This is a chance:

- to reassure people. 'I don't anticipate any big changes as far as you're concerned, John, but of course I shall be making every effort to help you make your performance even better';
- to stroke. 'Penny Smith told me what a great job you did for her on the Acme report. I know I can depend on you to carry on the good work';
- to impress. Not necessarily with your cleverness but with your sincerity, your availability and your willingness to help individual team members;
- to assess. If you have done your homework you will already know something about the individual members of your department. This first face-to-face meeting enables you to make your own provisional judgement. Don't neglect your instinct. Although it is far from infallible there is a good chance that your instinctive judgement will turn out to be correct.

ASSESSING PROCESSES

Even if you have been appointed as a 'trouble-shooter' you should give yourself a little time to assess the situation at first hand. If you have taken over an average or good department you can allow yourself more time to settle in before you begin making changes. Give yourself a chance to evaluate tasks, processes and material resources in the same way that you get to know your staff. Are the processes working? Will drastic changes be needed?

KEEP A RECORD

Before you take over you should have some information on the organization you are joining, the tasks of your new department and the material and human resources you will have to work with.

Use this as a basis for your filing system, adding information as you acquire it.

Use a cassette recorder to fix your observations and impressions each time you return to your own office. The first day, for example, will provide much useful information about the department and its morale. For example:

- are working areas tidy?
- do your people look smart, alert, confident and happy?
- do they have a 'can do' attitude?
- do they have a team spirit?

At the end of the first week you should be in a position to make a provisional 'management audit', listing the good and the bad things you have noted about your department and its people. Add to this and keep it up to date throughout your settling-in period, then keep it as a yardstick by which to measure the results of any improvements you have made.

Remember that you will wish much of this information to be confidential.

CHECK THE INVENTORY

You have a lot to think about but it makes sense to be certain that the items for which you are responsible really are where they are supposed to be. Check the equipment inventory if there is one and, if none exists, establish one. Otherwise, you could find yourself responsible for, say, the word processor that Jim Endersby – now long gone – took home to do a report.

MAKING FRIENDS

Take time to call on as many of your fellow front-line managers as possible, especially those who are the internal customers of your department. Don't go into detail at this stage but make sure that they and their secretaries know your name and new position; assure them of your wish to co-operate.

Other people with whom you should establish friendly relations are:

- doormen and receptionists. Make sure for a start that they know your name and position. They are often your first contact with the outside world. They can be marvellously effective allies but don't get on the wrong side of them unless you don't really want to get your parcels and messages the same day;
- telephone operators. Wonderful people! Again, make sure they know your name and position from day one. Get them on your side and you have acquired a message service, a secretarial agency, an intelligence network and a research bureau. Offend them and you and the people who call you could go on permanent 'hold';
- secretaries. Often one of the first tests of your people skills. It will take you a while to get to know your secretary's strengths and weaknesses.
  As a new manager you may have inherited a Dragon. Let this monster bully you a little until you find your feet and the Mr or Ms Perfect you took over from begins to be forgotten. Then have a chat about what a great team you are going to make, with lots of praise for the quality of the

work you have seen so far: 'I'm sure that you have lots of ideas about improvements we could make in the way we work together. Why don't you get them down on paper and we'll look at them and see what can be done.'

Remember, most secretaries like to think of themselves as personal assistants. Take things slowly at first but, if your secretary is capable of assisting you and is not going to take advantage of the situation or play favourites, you should encourage the development of their full potential as a team player.

SUMMARY

- Why you should see your new job as an opportunity to change – *yourself*.
- A rule of thumb for setting priorities. Things you can *control*, things you can *influence* and those that are largely *academic*.
- The manager's joke syndrome – or why everything you say or do now counts double.
- How to manage old friends and why this is usually less of a worry than you imagine.
- The 'softly softly' approach and what you need to know before making changes.
- Taking over from Superman, Wonderwoman or an unsuccessful manager.
- How to turn the runner-up for your job into your Number Two.
- Why you should establish a take-over 'audit' *and* check the inventory.
- Why you should make friends with the real VIPs like receptionists, doormen, telephone operators and, of course, your secretary.

PART TWO

Leadership

THREE

Leading from the Front

On the day you move up you acquire one of the most important attributes of management in the form of confirmed authority. From now on you are the boss – and it's official.

In fact, you may well have been given some tangible indication of your status in the shape of a reserved parking space or an office with your name on the door. You will almost certainly have been given a title which announces that you are in charge of a specific department and responsible for its performance.

Trivial though they may be in themselves, these minor 'trappings' of authority are important as outward signs that you are no longer a member of the rank and file and that, although your position may be relatively lowly and your powers restricted, your authority is backed by the management hierarchy.

As a new manager this authority means that the people who report to you will consider themselves bound by the 'psychological' contract – implied by the acceptance of employment and reinforced by habit and custom – to carry out your instructions. This is a very important feature of management, so much so that, until recently, together with some ability to organize, it was thought to be all that managers needed. The boss was the boss and that was that.

Today, however, because the managerial profession as a whole has been upgraded to match the capabilities of a better educated workforce, new managers are required to lead as well as to administer.

THE MANAGER AS LEADER

In the days when leaders led, managers managed and the rank and file did as they were told, leadership was regarded as an art, management was a science and work was a matter for 'rude mechanicals'.

Leadership was largely the province of the military and, as General Slim put it when Governor-General of Australia, the leader and those who followed him had 'one of the oldest, most natural and most effective of human relationships', while managers and the managed were 'a later product with neither so romantic nor so inspiring a history'. Leadership, was 'of the spirit, compounded of personality and vision, its practice an art', while management was 'more a matter of accurate calculation of statistics, of methods, timetables and routine, its practice was a science'.

THE TEMPORARY LEADERS

Curiously enough, it was the hidebound British military who – admittedly because they were forced to do so – introduced the concept of leadership as an essential quality for all those respons- ible for the performance of others, whatever their rank.

Because of its complexity, warfare on the huge scale of the two world wars called for thousands of leaders and the difficulty of providing them was compounded by enormous officer casu- alties.

In World War I, the solution was to commission 'temporary gentlemen' who were officer material rather than officer class but who, to many people's surprise, showed great qualities of leadership. However, in spite of this, most of them were content to revert to their original status once the fighting was over and the Army could get on with some 'real soldiering'.

The fact was that most of them were forced to do so because the short-sighted industrialists and businessmen of the day saw no need for leaders and considered that they were being generous if they gave the returning heroes their old jobs back.

THE NEW LEADERS

In World War II, after the often gallant blundering of the 'real' soldiers had once again revealed the need for large numbers of leaders, thousands of officers were promoted from the ranks of those entering Britain's 'Citizens' Army'.

By this time, however, the citizenry had changed to the sort of people who were no longer content to 'do or die' without asking the reason why. Their new officers, and in many cases the new NCOs, were expected to lead and were taught to do so.

Once again, the new leaders did well, but this time when peace came most of them were reluctant to abandon their hard-won status. Many of them took jobs in industry where, after a while, their leadership skills were appreciated and it was then that leadership began to be accepted as an important factor in management.

At the same time, many of those people who had been responsible for selecting and training leaders in wartime started to introduce similar methods into the selection and training of managers, providing new impetus for the managerial revolution.

THE MARRIAGE OF ART AND SCIENCE

The recognition of leadership as an important function of management means that the sort of management you, as a new manager, are required to practise today is a marriage of art and science. As General Slim put it, managers must be 'not only skilled organizers but inspired and inspiring leaders'.

Of course, the need to be an 'inspired and inspiring' leader may seem a little remote if you have just been made office supervisor or shop foreman, but leadership is vital in all grades of management and the fact that you have direct contact with the rank and file makes your first management position an ideal training ground.

LEADERS – BORN OR MADE?

The Army's new ideas on leadership, as subsequently developed by civilian theorists and practitioners, provide a solution to the worries of many new managers who are concerned that they may not be 'born' leaders.

In fact, experience has demonstrated that the innate qualities of leadership are fairly distributed throughout the population in much the same way as an aptitude for music.

Of course, there are people who have little aptitude for leadership just as there are people who are unmusical. Equally obviously, those who have leadership aptitudes will benefit from being educated as leaders in much the same way that a child with an aptitude for music will benefit from being brought up in a musical household.

However, just as being brought up in a musical family will not help a tone-deaf child to become a good musician, being brought up among leaders will not make a child without leadership aptitudes a good leader. This means that, although some people may have more aptitude for leadership than others, there is no such thing as a 'born' leader.

In other words, leadership is a factor which you as a new manager can control. Your move up to management is a vote of confidence in your leadership potential which you are now able to develop. You can *learn* to be a leader and even decide what sort of leader you wish to be.

As Buck Rogers, who was Vice-President of Marketing at IBM in its heyday, put it, 'I don't think anyone is a born leader. A person who aspires to a high managerial position can develop the necessary skills if he or she is ambitious and dedicated enough.'

LEARNING TO BE A LEADER

The best way to learn how to be a good leader is by leading and in *The Action Centred Leader* management training specialist John Adair uses the model of three overlapping circles to emphasize that leaders must be guided by the three shared needs of working groups:

- the need to accomplish a common task;
- the need to be maintained as a team;
- the sum of the group's individual needs.

As a new manager you may well find yourself at the head of a team of people who are doing unglamorous and perhaps repetitive jobs. As a leader you must be able to earn their trust and respect, and try to inspire them with enthusiasm for their task. Good leadership can make people more willing to tackle unglamorous tasks and if you can do this you need have no doubts about your ability to lead.

DEVELOPING LEADERSHIP QUALITIES

Within limits, it is possible for front-line managers to decide what sort of leader they will be and, in most cases, their control over this aspect of management increases as they achieve seniority. However, there are some constant leadership qualities which are needed, whatever your style, and many of these have high *control* and *influence* quotients.

Good leaders:

- *Provide a role model.* Managers who wish their people to be smartly turned out, punctual, hard-working, considerate, innovative, loyal and so on, must demonstrate these qualities themselves. Most employees, for example, find it hard to work well for a boss who habitually returns to the office 'tired and emotional' after a three-hour lunch.
- *Have a plan.* As a leader you must make it clear that you know what you are doing and where you are going. As a junior manager you may often find yourself implementing somebody else's plan. Don't knock it or disclaim responsibility for it. Fight it out with your superiors if you disagree with it but, once you have had your say, accept it as *the* plan, fine-tune it if possible, and then do your best to get your people to make it work.
- *Are decisive.* All managers make decisions. The mark of a good leader is that, while he is prepared to listen to others where appropriate and if there is time to do so, he is also able to make even unpleasant decisions quickly and firmly.
- *Project enthusiasm and optimism.* Both are contagious and

29

people will be prepared to follow you if you show that you believe in yourself and your ideas.

- *Accept responsibility.* Your people must be confident that you accept total responsibility for the performance of the group's tasks and that you will not try to blame them for your mistakes.
- *Are visible.* Good leaders practise what has come to be known as 'Management by Walking About'. This almost symbolic gesture involves leaving the 'safety' of your office to talk to – and listen to – the troops in their own work stations. Apart from improving communications, this provides an opportunity to observe, to give encouragement and to 'stroke' where appropriate. *Visibility* is especially important in times of crisis when the true leader is not only visible but actively helpful.
- *Walk about – don't stalk about.* Visible management must be positive. People should be glad to see you as you approach their work station, smile and greet them by name. This is the time you pick up feedback about your leadership and find out if people are prepared to talk to you (which is good) and make suggestions (which is better). Praise in public, but reprimand in private. Don't take over 'private' space by, for example, sitting on their desks without asking permission. You are a guest in their 'comfort zone', not an invasion force.
- *Take a genuine interest in their people.* In action, officers eat only after they have made sure that the troops have been fed. The welfare and well-being of the people who report to you both in the workplace and away from it should be one of your major concerns as a manager.
- *Are courteous and considerate.* 'Manage as you would be managed' is a good rule of thumb and many successful leaders, like former international construction manager Bernard Lauvergeat, believe it to be the cardinal rule of management. 'When making decisions,' says Lauvergeat, 'especially those affecting individuals, I used to think back to the days when I was a working engineer and ask myself how I would have responded.'

- *Know when to be firm.* People like to know where they stand and how far they can go, so good leaders make sure that the ground rules are clear and that everyone knows they will be enforced. You will earn more leadership points by being vigilant than by allowing yourself to be taken in by workplace manipulators.
- *Remain cool if there is a crisis.* Easier said than done perhaps, but panic is contagious so you must provide an example of cool, unruffled efficiency.
- *Have the ability to build up a team, to motivate it and to delegate tasks to its members.* These are important branches of the art of leadership which we shall look at separately.

A QUESTION OF STYLE

As a new manager, it is almost certain that your leadership style will be influenced by the culture of the organization you work for but, even in the most structured systems, individuals usually have a certain amount of leeway.

As a rule your control of this particular leadership factor will be based on your results and the results of your team. Remember the story of the chief executive officer of a large American company whose right-hand man asked, 'What on earth should I do about Doug Brown? He spends more time on the golf course than in the office, turns up late for appointments, dresses like a hippy and allows the whole of the workforce to call him Doug'.

'Sounds like a problem,' agreed the CEO, 'but what are his results like?'

'Well,' answered the assistant, 'as a matter of fact his division has the best record of any in the group. Production is up, absenteeism is way down and, although he seems to regard money as something to be shovelled out of moving trains, somebody in his team must be keeping a careful eye on costs.'

'Right,' said the CEO. 'Here's what you do. Fire the heads of all the other divisions and recruit another set exactly like Doug.'

Whatever works is usually the right style but a great deal depends on who you are leading and it takes a different style to lead, say, a team of brain surgeons than it does to head a nunnery or run a building site.

LEARN FROM THE GREAT LEADERS

The best thing to do is to evolve a style of your own based on your own personality and incorporating some of the things you admire and consider appropriate in the style of great leaders of the past or successful business leaders of today.

As a new manager, for instance, while it is highly unlikely that you will be faced like the mortally wounded Sir Philip Sidney, the Elizabethan soldier-poet, with a choice between drinking a proffered cup of water or giving it up to a dying soldier, there will be times when a thy-need-is-greater-than-mine attitude will demonstrate your leadership qualities.

In much the same way, if you are asked to take over a demoralized department, you could do a lot worse than refer to the ways in which, according to Shakespeare, Henry V revitalized the bedraggled and outnumbered English army at Agincourt with a rousing eve of battle speech or examine how, in World War II, General Montgomery turned round a defeated and broken Eighth Army when he took command two months before the battle of El Alamein.

Montgomery's 'We are going to finish with this chap Rommel' address to his staff officers, in which he told them of his intention to stand and fight, assured them of his confidence in them and their ability to work as a team and told them 'if anyone thinks it can't be done, let him go at once' is a masterpiece of leadership in action with plenty of opportunity for what has been called 'constructive swiping'.

Closer to home, business leaders like the innovative and massively successful Body Shop boss Anita Roddick or the flamboyant Julian Richer, the founder and owner of Richer Sounds, can provide useful pointers. Richer, whose country house is available for staff holidays and who sends a Rolls Royce for the use of his most successful branch, believes in 'keeping the buzz going' and providing rewards and lots of recognition – all things you can incorporate into your managerial style, even if you don't have a Rolls.

Good leaders are role-players who have decided in advance which role will suit them and the best leaders are those who are able to adapt their style to the people they lead and to circumstances.

HOW WILL YOU KNOW YOU HAVE SUCCEEDED?

Results, of course, are a good measure of your success as a manager and have the advantage of being quantifiable but, if your people are happy to introduce you to their friends, their family and strangers with 'This is my boss', you will know that you have succeeded as a leader.

SUMMARY

- Authority – or what you get, along with your new title and an office with your name on the door.
- The psychological contract and why most employees will be predisposed to do as you ask.
- How managers changed to become leaders as well as administrators and management became a marriage of art and science.
- The myth of the 'born' leader and how you can *learn* to lead.
- Leadership qualities and how to develop them.
- Leadership style, the managerial role and how to adapt your style to suit the people you are leading, the circumstances and, usually, your track record.
- Learning from great leaders and how to 'swipe' leadership ideas from victorious generals and successful business pioneers.

FOUR

The Magic of Teams

One of the most exciting and satisfying things that can happen to you once you move up to management is to discover that, thanks to your leadership, the group of people for whom you are responsible has become a team, a living entity with an energy of its own.

Of course, if you are lucky, your whole organization will be one big team with your CEO as its chief coach, presiding over a series of interlocking teams of senior, middle and front-line managers.

As a front-line manager you will probably have little or no control of the corporate team, although you may be able to influence it as a member of your immediate superior's team and perhaps as a member of teams made up of your fellow-managers.

As far as team-building is concerned, your real control will be over the people who report to you and who you can organize and inspire.

Naturally, a great deal will depend on the sort of team you have inherited and the scope of your authority, but it is safe to assume that, as a new manager, you will not have been appointed to manage the equivalent of a First Division football team or have unlimited financial resources for recruiting new 'players'. However, as a manager, you should have some authority to hire and fire staff, in which case a sound rule, once you have settled in, is to *hire the best, train the rest and get rid of the pest* until you have a team in which all the members are pulling in the same direction.

TEAM BUILDING AND SYNERGY

It is this unity of purpose which gives rise to the phenomenon of *synergy* (a term derived from the Greek for 'together' and 'work'), which enables teams to defy the laws of ordinary mathematics. Thanks to synergy, two and two can make five, as the effect of two or more people working together is greater than the sum of the effects of the same number of individuals working separately.

If you have ever played in, or supported, an 'unbeatable' sports team you will have no difficulty in recognizing the presence of synergy. It's 'magic', which is why persuading people to work together towards a common aim is one of the most important functions of management of all grades.

WHEN TWO AND TWO MAKE THREE

As a front-line manager you are more likely than managers of higher grades to come across groups of people who are not yet efficiently functioning teams. You could then experience the phenomenon of negative synergy, which is what happens when the disruptive effect of two or more people acting together is greater than the sum of the disruption they would cause as individuals.

This is where you as the leader have to move in to 'get rid of the pest', not necessarily by firing the people concerned – although, in the final resort, this may be your only possible course – but by splitting up disruptive groups and moving people to other sections.

MOVES AND TRANSFERS

Like the manager of a football team, you can leave those people who are happy and effective in their current positions, while moving others, especially those who say they would like a change, and matching up individuals with the jobs they can do best. By using this sort of interior recruitment within your team and directing square pegs into square holes, you will encourage multi-skilling and could even discover a couple of stars.

If you are still not satisfied that you have best mix of talent and ability you could try a couple of voluntary 'free transfers' with other departments, in much the same way as a football manager might swap an unhappy player for one who is dissatisfied with his current team.

As a new manager you should find that this method of team-building has a high control factor as it is relatively inexpensive. The only alternative, apart from leaving things as they are, is to fire the no-hopers and replace them, perhaps with younger people whose enthusiasm and willingness to learn may compensate for their lack of experience.

HIRE THE BEST – FOR YOU

If you are able to hire staff, either as replacements or additions, the main criteria should be the individual's competence and their possible effect on your team and, while you could need someone to shake up a team which is becoming complacent, your usual requirement will be for someone who will 'fit in'.

When you interview a candidate you should have already had a chance to study their application, their c.v. and, in the case of an internal application, their record.

When you begin the interview, although a couple of minutes' chat to put the candidate at ease is well worth while, it's usually a mistake to embark on a detailed description of the position in question as, besides giving candidates a chance to frame their answers to fit your requirements, it could be a waste of time, should you decide to cut the interview short.

Although your priorities may vary, you need to know about the candidate's professional experience, their education and training, together with something about their personal life. One way of organizing the interview is to write down parallel lists, one stating your requirements and the other how the candidate fulfills them. As a rule, you should persuade the candidate to do 80 per cent of the talking while you do 20 per cent. You can do this by avoiding questions which call for a 'Yes' or 'No' answer in favour of such questions as, 'Tell me what you were doing in your last job' or 'How would you go about tackling a client who is a persistently late payer?'.

Hiring is an important part of team-building as it has a high control quotient. Hiring successfully reflects credit on your abilities and, if you are fortunate, can instil a feeling of loyalty in the candidate you choose.

HOW MANY IN A TEAM?

While there is no hard and fast rule about the optimal number of individuals in any given team, four to six people are usually enough to provide the benefits of synergy, while any more than 12 will begin to be unwieldy. Many teams, including sports teams, appear to have more than 12 members but, in fact, both on the sports field and in the workplace, such teams break down naturally into subsidiary teams based on specialist roles.

Within your main team, as well as these 'natural' teams, you will almost certainly create several task-orientated teams, either as part of your own plan or in order to implement management initiatives.

A COMMON GOAL

Whatever the size and composition of these teams, the best way to ensure positive synergy is to provide them with a common goal. However, the goal must be achievable and, if it is a long-term objective, there should be plenty of short-term goals along the way.

For example, it would be worse than useless for the manager of a struggling 'home-grown' football team to announce to his players that the team's goal was the FA Cup. Giant Killers *have* reached Wembley Stadium but, in practice, no matter what his ambitions, the manager would be better off setting promotion to a higher division as a long-term goal, with a number of short-term goals along the way – starting with winning the next match.

In the workplace, your long-term goal might be to eliminate waste completely, but the intermediate goal you set your team would be to cut waste by, say, 10 per cent. You should also arrange to reward individual and team efforts in achieving intermediate goals, if only by recognition and 'stroking'.

TRAINING TO WIN

People love to win, and one advantage of team-building is that it provides a chance for everyone to win without causing anyone to lose, as the team's 'victories' will usually involve beating targets or deadlines. Creating opportunities for this sort of win will help your people to appreciate the value of training, which is one of the many things that you as manager will need to sell to them.

Of course, the need to train every member of your staff to achieve his or her full potential is blindingly obvious to *you* but, like many other things you will come across in your new role, it may not be quite so crystal-clear to your staff. Explain how *they* will benefit as individuals and as a team rather than what you and the company will get out of it.

Involve your experienced people in training the others. Almost everybody enjoys teaching others by demonstrating their own skills.

PICKING TEAMS

Selecting members of task-specific teams means choosing people who are capable of doing the job and should include a leader, an ideas person, an administrator and a 'driver' to push the others along.

You could think of them as providing inspiration, ratiocination, organization and galvanization and, translated into real-life shop floor or office terms, the team's role-players might turn out to be people like:

- Mike – who frequently says such things as, 'Come on. Let's do it like this,' and gets his own way most of the time;
- Maurice – the clever, knowledgeable chap who is always thinking of better ways to do things;

- Margaret – who is meticulous and a bit bossy but likes keeping records and organizing;
- Jack – who is a bundle of energy and hates to see anyone standing still.

TYPECASTING

If your organization is a large one, you could get some help in picking people for specific team roles from the results of psychological tests they have taken, but it is best to regard these as guidelines only and to make your own assessment.

People have been trying to classify their fellow human beings for centuries and one recent system, based on the three main physical types (endomorphs, who are plump to fat; mesomorphs who are average; and ectomorphs who are thin) harks back to Shakespeare's 'Oh, let me have men about me that are fat'.

Again, the astrological 'star signs', while they may lack precision when it comes to foretelling the future, provide a useful way of identifying 12 different types of person and you could find yourself saying things like, 'What that team really needs is a Taurus'.

Whatever system of classification you use, identifying psychological types will help you to predict how people are likely to react to any given set of circumstances, to decide on their tasks and team roles, and indicate how best to coach them.

THE LIFE STORY OF THE TEAM

The teams you create to enable you to carry out your tasks are living entities which, once they are formed, go through an – often turbulent – adolescence, then mature, grow old and die, a process which managers can control to some extent, but appears to be inevitable.

One way of expressing this life cycle is to define the stages as: forming, storming, norming and performing – followed eventually by deforming.

- *Forming*. The time of choosing individual members, giving the team an identity, often symbolized by a name or logo, and allotting roles.

- *Storming*. The stage corresponding to adolescence is often a time when individuals jockey for position, a time of challenges, disputes and insecurity. It is also a time of enthusiasm and optimism.
- *Norming*. The settling down stage when the leader, the ideas person, the administrator and the driver begin to assert themselves. This is when new ideas are adopted and put into practice.
- *Performing*. The 'mature' stage when the team is working exactly as it should and with the maximum synergetic effect. Because it is the most productive stage there is a temptation to force people to reach it quickly, but teams need time to grow and develop while individual members gain confidence in themselves and their group. When the team is working well, managers need to motivate it to improve performance and to maintain it at this productive stage for as long as possible.
- *Deforming*. The equivalent of old age. The symptoms include self-satisfaction and resistance to new ideas. The workplace 'comfort zone' with its traditions, jargon and cameraderie becomes a stultifying exclusion zone whose members are fearful of strangers and change.

One way in which managers can prolong the life of teams is by introducing new members – if possible before the group becomes too exclusive. New members almost always put the team back in its Forming-Performing sequence so that the group begins 'storming' all over again. There's nothing quite like it for revitalizing a team that has almost reached its die-by date and it's worth putting up with a second adolescence to give your team a new lease of productive life.

DIFFERENT TEAMS FOR DIFFERENT MATCHES

In most cases the department you take over will already be divided into more or less permanent teams, each of which is responsible for a part of the overall task. Provided such teams are already performing well, there should be no need for personnel changes apart from bringing in the occasional new member. However, you may decide to create, or be asked to create, teams to tackle specific problems by making use of the knowledge and experience of every member of the group, and for this sort of team you can co-opt team members who are 'experts' in the area under consideration from among the whole of your staff.

HANDS UP – WHO'D RATHER BE IN A MEETING?

We shall be discussing ways in which these teams can be motivated later, but for the moment it is worth remembering that you should keep the team's purpose in mind at all times. When meetings are held, make sure that you get a copy of the agenda beforehand and a copy of any notes that are circulated after the team meets. One reason for this is that, although meetings are inexpensive and effective, they do cost money in terms of wages and can even hold up production by taking people away from their work. In addition, as meetings are often more fun than everyday work, there is a temptation to hold more of them than are needed.

All you need to do is to make it clear that you wish to be informed about the dates and composition of meetings and to be given a summary of what transpires. This should save you from walking into a section of your department and finding that it has unexpectedly turned into an industrial *Marie Celeste*.

PRACTISE LEADING

Maintain control by leading some teams yourself and by appointing the leaders of the rest. Get the whole team moving in the same direction by setting attainable objectives and by using other methods of motivation – a topic important enough to warrant separate treatment as a distinct art of leadership.

New managers should make an effort to lead one or two of the teams they set up. This is not only a good way of getting feedback from their staff but is also useful practice for the times when they are called on as members of managerial or inter-disciplinary teams.

SUMMARY

- Build teams *you* control.
- Hire the best, train the rest and get rid of the pest – but not necessarily by firing them.
- The magic of synergy and how to make sure it works *for* you.
- Team-building by moves and transfers.
- Keeping control of the job interview to make sure you hire the best for you and your team.
- Prevent teams being unwieldy – create teams within your team.
- Follow the team-building formula and make sure of the mix.
- Typecasting – your team's future in the stars.
- The life story of the team and how to extend its peak performance.
- Beware of having too much of a good meeting.
- Why you should lead some of your teams yourself.

FIVE

Teamworking

Working together as a team is a concept you may have to sell to your staff, many of whom will have been taught throughout most of their school lives that taking advantage of their classmates' skills and ideas is a crime.

Few of them will remember the class projects of their early schooldays when they worked together as a team to achieve a common goal. Instead, they will have been conditioned by the competitive, senior class approach which demanded that everything they did should be 'all their own work'.

In this frame of mind, while they may be happy to form teams and to attend team meetings, their achievements could be minimal.

Your job is not only to form them into teams but to take them back to their junior school days when class projects supervised by teachers taught them how to co-operate.

As good managers, good teachers were actively involved in initiating class projects, were available to provide advice and backup, and retained overall control even though the class 'owned' the task. Projects were fun but they were not allowed to get out of hand. Now, you are the 'teacher' and your job is to get your teams interested and involved while making certain that they keep the team's aims in mind.

TEAMS ARE NOT COMMITTEES

There's an old saying that the camel is 'a horse designed by a committee' but, in fact, the camel is perfect for its environment and could have been designed by a first-class team, while a committee would have come up with something resembling a duckbilled platypus.

Teams are not committees, nor are they debating societies, social gatherings or discussion groups. They are a means of involving a number of individuals whose varied skills and talents are needed to achieve a common goal. Teamwork is fun but 'work' is an important component of the word and structuring and controlling teams doesn't make teamwork any less enjoyable.

KEEP CONTROL

As we stressed when discussing team-building, the composition of teams will vary according to their task, which may involve improving a process, generating ideas, or solving problems. Whatever their function, all teams must have a team leader who, apart from the times you elect to lead the team yourself, will be either appointed or approved by you.

In a workplace where enthusiasm is running high, team projects may be suggested by staff who may also put forward ideas on who should be team leader. However, while such initiatives are a tremendous breakthrough and a tribute to your leadership abilities, you should still make it clear that you have the final say on both counts. Usually, of course, you will then accept this evidence of co-operation gracefully – and gratefully.

Involvement is an excellent way to maximize the contribution of individuals towards the attainment of a common goal but it should not imply the abdication of managerial control.

THE QUALITIES AND TASKS OF THE TEAM LEADER

If you do not elect to lead the team yourself, the team leader you appoint should be capable of enthusing and guiding the other members of the team. He or she should also be expert in those areas to be considered by the team.

With your guidance where appropriate, the team leader should:

- select the members of the team, bearing in mind the qualities each person will be required to bring to the team task;
- set dates for team meetings;
- allocate responsibilities and co-ordinate the team's activities;
- monitor progress by keeping records or arranging for them to be kept;
- keep you, as front-line manager, informed about the team's progress.

PREPARING FOR A TEAM MEETING

The team leader's preparations should include:

- deciding on, and where necessary booking, the venue;
- arranging for the provision of such equipment as pencils and notepads, flipcharts and video recorders;
- arranging for refreshments, where appropriate, and checking on availability of toilet facilities;
- reviewing the above points with the immediate superior and discussing any 'warm up' exercises which may be necessary, together with any other ways in which people can be motivated to participate fully;
- notifying team members in plenty of time for them to re-adjust their schedules.

THE FIRST MEETING

At the beginning of the first meeting members should decide, with the guidance of the team leader:

- who is going to take notes;
- who will be responsible for the distribution of agendas;
- how long it should take before the minutes of meetings are distributed;
- what happens if people are late, or don't turn up;
- how the team will handle interruptions like 'phone calls or pagers.

As front-line manager you are responsible for briefing your teams and acting as senior coach by evaluating progress and being available to advise on any problems which may arise. In this way you should be able to strike a balance between enabling and controlling. Control can be less visible as soon as teams prove themselves by reaching the 'performing' stage.

USING TEAMS TO SOLVE PROBLEMS

Good managers don't worry. They know that worry can kill both them and their projects, while problem-solving is one of the most satisfying functions of management. As a front-line manager, when a problem is put forward, the ball is firmly in your court.

This is not to say that worries do not occur, but it does mean that in most cases listing the symptoms and causes of worries is sufficient to turn them into problems capable of solution, often by enlisting the help of teams.

Problems may arise during the day-to-day working of your department or they may come about in the course of implementing your own initiatives or those of senior management. Whether you decide to tackle the problem yourself, or to draw on the abilities of a team, it usually pays to follow a precise sequence of steps.

THE PROBLEM-SOLVING PROCESS

1. Identify the problem and understand it.
2. Identify likely cause of the problem.
3. Put forward and analyse possible solutions.
4. Plan the intended action.
5. Take action.
6. Monitor results.
7. Evaluate results and amend the plan where necessary.

TEAMS AND THE PROBLEM-SOLVING PROCESS

A glance at the above steps indicates that a correctly chosen team can in effect 'own' the problem. Because they are closer to their particular process than you are, they will usually be in a better position to identify it, to understand its implications and to pin-point likely causes. In some cases they may even have brought the problem to your attention.

For the same reason they will be well placed to plan the action to be taken and, after consulting you, to act. They will also be able to monitor the results and, guided by you, to amend the plan before acting again.

MOTOR MANAGEMENT

The seven steps towards problem-solving outlined above can be repeated until a satisfactory solution has been found and many of the steps can be further divided into other sequences so that you could, for instance, use the teamworking technique called *brainstorming* to discover the team's ideas on possible solutions to the problem.

However, in the first instance, a great many management processes, especially where problem-solving is concerned, can be simplified to a four-step sequence which – using the analogy of the basic combustion engine – we call *motor management*.

The name emphasizes the continuous nature of management processes with its repetition of *Planning, Acting, Controlling, Acting* – the initial letters of which make the appropriate mnemonic: PACA PACA PACA PACA.

By repeating the PACA sequence you will achieve the sort of improvement which the Japanese call Kaizen or 'continuous improvement involving everyone' and which Emile Coué propounded many years before them as 'Every day, in every way, I am becoming a little better'.

USING MOTOR MANAGEMENT

Adding to the PACA PACA sequence should give you a more efficient, smoother running 'motor', but you should be careful about 'bolt-on goodies' which do little or nothing to move things along.

In emergencies, the PACA PACA sequence indicates a straightforward course of action which is easy to follow and makes for rapid solutions. Thinking of teamworking in the light of a simple motor suggests that, as well as making the PACA PACA sequence more sophisticated, you, as manager, can also steer, accelerate and apply the brakes. After all, you are responsible for guiding your department 'vehicle' to its designated destination, at the best possible speed and without mishap.

GUIDING AND CONTROLLING THE MOTOR

Teams – like cars – need steering, acceleration and from time to time braking and, while too much regimentation can strangle initiative, proceeding 'in an orderly manner' is the essence of management. Managers who fail to guide and control their teams are as out of place as bumper car drivers on a Grand Prix circuit.

This is why even a teamwork process as apparently freewheeling and chaotic as *brainstorming* needs to be structured to some degree.

BRAINSTORMING

Brainstorming works by getting individuals in a team situation to come up with ideas, which trigger more ideas from the team, which in turn provoke more ideas, eventually creating a highly charged mental climate in which the team becomes an ideas generating machine. In order to allow this mental excitement to develop, brainstorming sessions need to be fairly informal and, unless managers and their team leaders are careful, this can lead to difficulties.

THE CASE OF THE BRAINLESS BRAINSTORMERS

Take the case of the young fellow who took over as editor of his university newspaper at a time when its circulation was at an all-time low. Realizing that he hadn't got the right team for the job, he managed to persuade most of the former editor's staff that they would not be happy working for the new, lively paper he envisaged. He then replaced them with a number of bright, would-be journalists who were brimful of talent and enthusiasm.

His first move was to get his staff to 'brainstorm' ideas for the new paper, making certain that there was plenty of liquid refreshment available to stimulate people's thought processes.

As far as generating ideas was concerned, the brainstorming session was a complete success, with projects for news coverage, features and layout becoming steadily more imaginative as the night wore on. The only trouble was that, on the following day, while everyone knew that 'hundreds' of brilliant ideas had been put forward, no one could remember much about any of them.

TAMING THE STORM

At the next brainstorming session the young editor solved this particular problem by appointing a virtually teetotal record keeper, but it was only by trial and error that he discovered how best to make brainstorming work by establishing a simple framework.

In order to get all the benefits of brainstorming without the disadvantages team leaders need:

- to appoint a record keeper;
- to give the team a specific topic to be brainstormed;
- to ask individual members of the team for ideas;
- to solicit ideas from the whole of the team;
- to record every idea.

Structuring brainstorming in this way makes it possible to use the technique without detracting from the team's fun.

USING BRAINSTORMING

Brainstorming can be used, for example, in the problem-solving process to identify problems, to analyse possible causes and to list possible solutions, with each stage treated as a separate brainstorming topic.

Humour reduces tensions and inhibitions in the team situation, so team leaders should allow it to develop naturally without getting out of hand.

Speed is essential. There's no such thing as a slow storm and brainstorming sessions should crackle with energy. Don't stop to criticize or evaluate ideas at this stage. The odd groan of mock despair or 'Wow!' of encouragement is permissible but otherwise, once the team is really brainstorming, it's best to keep the flow of ideas going.

IDEAS UNLIMITED

People often refrain from putting their ideas forward because of shyness. They fear their ideas are too unimportant to be of interest and that they will be ridiculed by their boss or their colleagues. These fears usually vanish in the heat of a brainstorming session as team members realize that the team leader is aiming for quantity and that all ideas are potentially valuable. However, you should make sure they know that the simplest ideas are often the best and that what you are really after is something like the suggestion that abrasive surfaces need only be put on one side of match boxes – an inspiration which saved match makers Bryant & May a fortune.

Make sure that everyone knows that you value *all* ideas, from the wildest to the most prosaic, because even an apparently 'useless' idea can lead to a new way of looking at a problem.

Warn team leaders to treat all ideas seriously and with courtesy. Making a tentative suggestion in the course of a brainstorming session may be the first sign of genuine interest in the job an individual has shown after remaining impervious to any number of management appeals.

One typical Health Service 'Jobsworth' character, who was renowned for his surly 'Can't be done – it's more than me job's worth' attitude, became a ball-of-fire innovator and the 'star' of his region's motivation campaigns once he realized that his ideas were being taken seriously and that he really did know more about some aspects of his job than his bosses.

Don't miss a chance to turn a cynical 'hand' into an enthusiastic employee, or an enthusiastic employee into a totally involved colleague.

THE 'SMALL' IDEAS CAMPAIGN

Motivation consultants IML Ltd solved the problem of people being reluctant to put forward 'unimportant' ideas by introducing a campaign called QED which calls not for world-shattering ideas but for practical 'wrinkles' which will save the employee's company a Quid Every Day. Properly motivated, almost everyone at the sharp end turns out to have a suggestion to contribute and in some cases companies have saved hundreds of thousands of quid, or pounds, a year.

MAKING BRAINSTORMING EFFECTIVE

At the end of a brainstorming session the team leader should be in a position to give you a list of all the ideas put forward. Send this back with a brief evaluation of each idea and a request that the team review any potentially valuable ideas in detail. You and they should then examine the control factor of each suggestion and list each one under the heading 'control', 'partial control' or 'no control'. For example:

- a suggestion to change the position of desks or machines might be within the control of the team;
- a suggestion to buy new equipment could be within your control;
- a suggestion to add office space or build a new workshop might be a 'no control' idea which you would need to evaluate and channel upward.

THE MANAGER AS A TEAM PLAYER

Even as a new manager you will almost certainly find yourself working as a member of teams composed of managers on the same grade as yourself or made up of specialists regardless of grade. Whatever the composition of the team, the principles remain the same and you should find the experience you have gained by creating teams and monitoring teamworking within your own department invaluable.

SUMMARY

- 'Selling' the teamwork concept.
- How teams differ from committees, debating societies and discussion groups.
- How to keep control of your teams; the role of the team leader; preparing for the first meeting; decisions to be made.
- Why good managers don't worry.
- Teams and the problem-solving process.
- 'Motor management', a simplified managerial sequence for emergencies and as a basis for more sophisticated sequences.
- 'Brainstorming' – how to organize brainstorming sessions and harness the power of the storm.
- Why you should encourage every member of a brainstorming team to put forward suggestions; management may have lofty ideas but a workshop or office 'wrinkle' can sometimes save thousands of pounds.
- The new manager as a player on other people's teams.

SIX

Self-Motivation

Motivating other people to do their job and do it well is one of the most important arts of management and, as a new manager, you will find it almost impossible to motivate others if you are not yourself highly motivated.

Motivation implies movement and when we say that it is the manager's job to motivate the staff we mean that it is the manager who has to get things moving. Obviously the original driving force needed to do this has to come from somewhere.

In fact, everything we experience motivates or moves us to a certain extent and in some direction.

However, the same factors do not motivate everyone in the same way or to the same extent. A sunny day, for example, can motivate us to get up early but a rainy day might do exactly the opposite, so that the weather as a motivating factor can be either positive or negative. At the same time, a sunny day might be highly motivating to most people, while a drought-stricken farmer whose land is turning into a dust bowl might find yet another day of sunshine demotivating.

In practice, as a manager you are unlikely to expose your staff to negative motivation. Instead, you will try to expose them to positive motivation and protect them from demotivation in order to persuade them, not merely to move, but to move in the direction you wish. We can mentally distinguish this positive motivation by thinking of it with a capital 'M' and at the same time use 'demotivation' to describe the effect of negative motivating factors.

Motivating with a capital 'M', which involves the deliberate introduction of motivating factors, has a high *control* quotient as it usually involves minimal expenditure and is extremely cost-effective. This makes it an attractive initiative for front-line managers.

In order to be able to motivate individual members of their staff, and to motivate their staff as a complete group or in teams, managers themselves need to be motivated and it is convenient to think of this in terms of 'self-motivation'.

SELF-MOTIVATION

Self-motivation is a useful way of describing the personal motivation leaders need if they are to motivate others, even though personal motivation is largely a question of the individual's reaction to motivating factors, including the motivating efforts of other people.

Looked at in this way, it is obvious that self-motivation has a high *control* quotient, because you can seek out those factors which motivate you positively and increase their effect.

As a new manager, for example, you can deliberately seek out factors like inspiration and challenges, while at the same time changing your conditioned responses to other motivating factors in a positive way by undergoing training, by reading or by meeting new people.

Like other leadership attributes, the ability to motivate oneself in this way is not the prerogative of any section of the population, although some people are more responsive to positive motivation factors than others. This is usually because they have more physical or mental energy and increasing your physical and mental energy is one aspect of self-motivation over which you have control.

MOTIVATION AND THE 'W' QUESTIONS

'I have five loyal serving men,' wrote Rudyard Kipling, 'their names are Who? What? Why? Where? When?', a mnemonic which rapidly became the basis of all young journalists' training and which has now become one of the workhorses of management.

We shall be coming across these 'W' questions many times

and with reference to many different aspects of management. Fortunately, the questions, like many of the formal sequences, which now we need to examine step by step, soon become second nature. Just as, when driving a car, experienced drivers no longer have to think about things like the gear changes they found so difficult while learning to drive, experienced managers move through complicated sequences automatically without missing a step.

Meanwhile, it is useful to follow sequences like Kipling's 'serving men' consciously and conscientiously. For example, before thinking in terms of self-motivation you should ask yourself the all-important 'W' questions about who, what, why, where and when you need to motivate, because moving up to management will have shifted your perspective and changed your attitude to many motivating factors.

Ask yourself:

- *Who* is the 'self' you need to motivate? This 'who' will be influenced by things like where you were born, your sex, your race, your family, your education and your career, together with your social and sporting history to date. These are the influences which have shaped you into the sort of person you are and your move up to management may well have as much influence on your character as any other single factor.

Becoming a manager is such an important career watershed that now is a good time to take stock of your 'culture' and its influence. Remind yourself, for example, of any prejudices you may have acquired along the way, any characteristics like greed or pride which may have come to exercise an undue influence. You should also review the things of which you feel you can be proud, like honesty, industriousness and so on.

Would you describe yourself as intelligent? Don't put too much faith in intelligence tests because people can be taught how to improve their scores in most of them. Don't confuse intelligence with the effects of cultural advantages due to things like family and education. If you have any doubts, remind yourself that you were judged intelligent enough to be promoted.

Are you ambitious or unambitious, impetuous or over-cautious, selfish or unselfish, greedy or generous? These and other traits are, to some extent, pre-dispositions we are born with but they are largely the result of conditioning – which means they can be changed. You have a lot of control over the 'self' you need to motivate.

- *What* do you need to motivate yourself to do? Up to now you have been a follower, at least in the workplace, but as a manager you have to motivate yourself to be a leader.

In practice, this means that you have to motivate yourself to work through other people in order to carry out the task assigned to you and, to do this, you may have to make considerable changes in your attitude and your methods of working.

- *Why* do you need to motivate yourself? You have to motivate yourself to become a motivating powerhouse to the point where you can provide other people with dynamic leadership for the whole of every working day. You need to be the driving force which gets everyone going, and this means you have to motivate yourself to expend a considerable amount of energy. In fact, your personal motivation has to be so strong that you are able to 'psych yourself up' to play the role of the inspired and inspiring leader, even when things are not going your way or when you are feeling down.

Leaders need to motivate themselves to become the sort of 'winners' who win by enabling other people to win and whose energy and enthusiasm will be contagious.

- *When* do you need to motivate yourself? As a manager you need to be motivated all the time, but the need for self-motivation becomes even more apparent in times of crisis or when deadlines have to be met.

Worse than a sudden crisis, however, is any sort of down-turn in the company's activities which, over a period, can sap the morale of management and workforce alike. It is at such times that you, as a front-line manager with direct and constant contact with the rank and file, will need to draw on all your reserves if you are to motivate yourself – and others.

- *Where* do you need to motivate yourself? Where you need to motivate yourself is something over which you exercised control when you accepted your new job. You may well have changed your environment when you moved up. However, even as a new manager, you can control some aspects of your working environment in such a way as to provide you with extra motivation, even if it is something as simple as re-arranging your office.

MOTIVE, MEANS AND OPPORTUNITY

When investigating crimes, detectives work on the principle that if they are to prove a suspect's guilt they must be able to show that he or she had a *motive* to commit the crime as well as the *means* and the *opportunity* to do so and that all three elements must be clearly established.

Shorn of its forensic association this formula is a useful one in many aspects of management. As a new manager, for instance, it is clear that you have been given the *opportunity* to do the job and, it must be hoped, the *means* to do it. You can now look at your *motives* for doing it, especially those which come under the heading of self-motivation.

THE HOW OF SELF-MOTIVATION

The answers to the 'W' questions determine the 'how' of self-motivation by indicating, for example, the long-range goals that you have set yourself. They enable you to establish how well you are motivated at the moment and how much you still need to motivate yourself.

In fact, all of us – the managers and the managed, the leaders and the led – are motivated by exactly the same groups of factors. Only the mix changes. A beggar and a banker will both be motivated by the need for food, but the beggar's need will almost certainly be greater than the banker's.

The sort of needs that motivate us are illustrated by Abraham Maslow's *Hierarchy of Needs*. Maslow (1908–70) asserted that people are motivated by a series of wants, ranging from the basic physiological needs for food, shelter and warmth to the higher needs like those for self-development, creativity and a 'noble cause', which he termed 'self-actualization' – meaning literally making yourself into a 'real' person.

Maslow's schematic representation of his theory in terms of a pyramid is still an excellent way of describing the groups of motivating factors and showing how they divide into 'lower' and 'higher' needs. However, Maslow argued that as each need is satisfied it vanishes, to be replaced by a higher one, but in fact satisfied needs, far from ceasing to motivate, remain potent. Anyone who has been hungry will still be motivated by the need for food and the fear of being unable to satisfy hunger, no matter how wealthy they may become.

HOW ARE YOU MOTIVATED NOW?

You are now in a position to list and quantify those factors which will motivate you in your new post and to establish a personal motivation audit.

Money will of course figure on your list, but how much are you motivated by it? How much are you motivated by your need for more of it? In the workplace, what are you prepared to do to get more of it? Would an extra £10,000 a year motivate you ten times as much as an extra £1,000 a year? How worried are you that you might lose your income?

How important is your new office? Are you motivated by the desire for an even better one?

Do you feel you are fitter and therefore better motivated in your new job, or do you find it stressful and therefore demotivating?

What about your family, if you have one? Do they help or hinder your self-motivation? For example, do they try to put you down or are they always ready to encourage you? Do you feel you can discuss any problems you may have in the workplace with your partner?

If you do have a family, it should provide a home 'comfort zone' for rest and relaxation, for solace when things are going wrong and for topping up your self-motivation. If you have a family that thinks you're the greatest – and says so – your personal motivation should be high.

How much of a motivator is your new status? Are you anxious to move up further and how would you feel if you were, for some reason, reduced to the ranks?

Job satisfaction should be a big motivating factor now you have achieved management status, have more responsibility and are dealing with the most interesting resource there is – people.

Do you feel that you are on your way to becoming a holistic 'winner', happy in your skin and certain that you are now developing as a human being? If so, you are finding self-actualizing factors motivating.

QUANTIFYING THE PYRAMID

Using the groups in the Maslow Pyramid, list all the factors that currently motivate you, marking the importance of each factor on a scale of nought to ten. In a separate column mark the factors you currently find demotivating, from nought to minus ten.

At the same time you could find it useful to note the *control* quotient of each factor, again on a scale of nought to ten. Which factors do *you* control?

The following outline will suggest factors which may be motivating you in a different way now you have moved up to management.

- *Physiological needs:*
1. Your job enables you to provide yourself – and family if you have one – with food, shelter, clothing, warmth. The move up to management, with its increase in salary, may make it possible to afford better accommodation etc.
2. If you are single, the new job, together with the prospect of further promotion, may widen your choice of partner.
3. The new job itself may have satisfied some of your

59

physiological needs. The trawler skipper, for example, who spends most of his working life on the enclosed bridge of his ship, rather than on the exposed deck, is highly motivated by his 'glass overcoat'.

- *Security needs:*
1. Moving up to management may well have increased your job security, perhaps because you now have a contract of employment.
2. More money will enable you to make better provision for security needs by acquiring savings, a pension, insurances and possessions.

- *Esteem needs:*
1. Your promotion should have increased the esteem in which you are held by your team and your superiors. It will certainly have increased your self-esteem.
2. As a manager, you are more 'visible' than formerly, which gives even your modest successes a high esteem rating.

- *Social needs:*
1. The fact that you are now in the 'people' business means that your working days will be filled with human contacts and transactions in which you will frequently be the person on whom the activity is centred.
2. You could derive many social satisfactions from meeting managers of your own grade, both in the workplace and outside it, especially as you will have common interests.

- *Self-actualization:*
1. Even as a new manager, you have more chance than before to become the 'real' you, to develop your personality, fulfil your potential and utilize your creative and innovative abilities.
2. As a manager, you are in a better position to help others and to have a goal that transcends yourself, even if at the moment it is only to make more and better widgets and to enable people to keep their jobs.

3. As a manager you have a chance to make a bigger contribution to the life of the community.

USING AUDITS

Once you have established your personal motivation audit, think about ways in which you can become more self-motivated. Keep the audit on file and make a second audit in, say, three months' time, in order to calculate the progress you have made. It doesn't matter how many motivating factors you list, as long as you keep the same list for the second and subsequent audits.

MONEY, MONEY, MONEY

You will have noticed that quite a few of the motivation factors mentioned above can be affected by the amount of money you have available, which makes this aspect of your promotion important.

The discovery – or, rather, the rediscovery – of the fact that there were other things in people's working lives besides money led some theorists to play down money as a motivating factor, but most of us are only too aware of its importance. As we have seen, more money helps take care of your physiological needs, your security needs, your social needs and to some extent your esteem needs. In addition, while it is not a prerequisite for self-actualization, it can oil the wheels, if only by making sure that the other needs are less of a problem.

Obviously, money is very important when you are young and need cash for house purchase and so on. However, as people grow older, other factors often do become more important, except for those who see money as a measure of success. As a new, and almost certainly young, manager you could find that money comes high on your list of motivating factors.

THE CONTROL QUOTIENT

The amount of Control you are able to exercise in this area should be high as, apart from money rewards, most of the decisions concerning your personal motivation and how to increase it will be yours. You will also be able to influence the extent to which other people are able to motivate you.

HOW WILL YOU KNOW YOU HAVE SUCCEEDED?

You will know that you have succeeded in becoming highly motivated if you find yourself eager to get to work and a little reluctant to leave, when you can't wait to get to grips with the problems of the day and to try out the ideas which you thought up while away from the workplace. Life for the highly motivated is fun for much of the time, both for the people concerned and for those round them.

SUMMARY

- Why you have to get *yourself* moving before you can begin to get things moving in the workplace.
- Everything motivates. Motivation is deliberate and positive. The leader's task is to motivate themselves, other individuals and groups of people.
- Why the 'self' you need to motivate changes when you move up to management and why this makes it a good time to take stock by asking the 'W' questions about your personal motivation: Who? What? Why? Where? When?
- The 'how' of personal motivation. How to motivate yourself by seeking out strongly motivating factors and, where necessary, by changing some of your cultural conditioning.
- Maslow's *Hierarchy of Needs*. What motivates you now you are a manager?
- How well-motivated a manager are you? How to quantify your personal motivation by establishing a motivation audit.
- Measuring improvement – and success.

SEVEN

Motivating Individuals

At first sight, motivating individual employees looks as though it ought to be much the same as self-motivation.

In fact, even though we are all motivated by the same factors, nothing could be further from the truth. This is because the answers to most of the 'W' questions (Who? What? Why? When? and Where?) are different, especially the answer to the question of who we need to motivate.

THE OTHER PERSON IS NOT YOU

Of course, it's perfectly obvious that other people are not us, so why do most of us insist on behaving as though they were and expecting them to react to things in exactly the same way as we do?

In spite of the evidence that we are each of us so different that out of several thousand million human beings none has the same fingerprints, we persist in treating other people as though they were bound to be motivated in exactly the same way as ourselves.

Ironically, most people find it easier to appreciate that the person they are dealing with is not exactly like them, if the individual in question is of a different race or sex. 'Ah,' they say, 'this person is patently different from me and may need to be motivated differently.' They are right – but for the wrong reasons. People do not always parade their 'cultural' differences, although sex and colour may sometimes be an indication of how people are motivated. In fact the greatest differences, and those most difficult to appreciate, may well be between people of the same sex, race and background.

Obviously, when it comes to motivating other people, the 'Do as you would be done by' rule, though still valid, needs some fine-tuning.

ASKING THE 'W' QUESTIONS

We can use the 'W' questions to decide *how* to motivate other individuals.

Imagine, for instance, that you want to motivate one of your staff to work harder, to improve the quality of their work or to put in some overtime.

- *Who?* If you have been doing your homework since 'moving in', especially if you have twelve people or fewer reporting to you, you should already know the person well. If not, you may have only a CV and a personnel file to go on.

Even the basic documentation will tell you a lot about the person you need to motivate. Indications of sex, race, creed, education and previous employment will allow you to make a preliminary assessment. It could well tell you what you should *not* do. A 'motivating' reward of a visit to a night club might not be suitable for someone whose CV shows them to be a lay preacher.

What you are looking for is the motivating factor, or factors, that individuals would choose themselves if they were in a position to do so. The documentation and direct contact with members of your staff should enable you to say with certainty, for example, if someone is a home body or would be highly motivated by the prospect of working abroad for a month.

- *What?* You should be absolutely clear in your own mind about what you want to motivate people to do before you ask them to come and see you.

The 'what?' needs to be specific. 'John, you are going to have to work a lot harder than you are doing at the moment' is demotivating compared to, 'John, what I think you should aim for is an increase of 5 per cent in the number of files you are processing.'

- *Why?* New managers should remind themselves that they need to motivate other individuals to ensure that the person concerned makes the optimum contribution to the work of the group. They need to do this because the function of management is to work through other people. In fact, *delegation* is so important that we have treated it separately (*see Chaps 9 & 10*).
- *Where?* Your office will usually be the best place to motivate individuals. Inviting someone into your territory stresses the importance you attach to the meeting.
- *When?* When you motivate people is an important consideration. Trying to motivate a member of your staff five minutes before they are due to leave work on Friday night is liable to be self-defeating.

HOW MUCH CAN YOU MOTIVATE?

You can motivate individual members of your staff on a continuous basis, as well as on specific occasions, and some of your motivation begins to operate as soon as they wake up in the morning. It may even have influenced their dreams and their sleep patterns. This makes it extremely important to motivate soundly and to avoid any demotivating factors.

In order to get an idea of how your motivation works at a distance and outside working hours, imagine that you are one of your staff who has just woken up in the morning.

It is a working day and ideally he or she has to be motivated to get out of bed, wash, dress, have breakfast, etc., travel and put in a day's work, employing all their skill and energy.

Motivating	*Demotivating*
sunny day	cold and raining
have slept well	sleep disturbed, nightmares (*C*)
smell of coffee	no sign of breakfast
partner in sunny mood	partner worried and anxious (*I*)
no real money worries	money worries, unpaid bills (*C*)

65

pleasant journey in prospect	more and more traffic jams
attractive approach	untidy surroundings (*I*)
attractive workplace	miserable workplace (*C*)
friendly ambience	grumpy workmates (*C*)
security	fear (*C*)
interesting work	dull, boring, repetitive work (*I*)
great boss, a pleasure to work for	rotten manager (*C*)

Add any other motivating and demotivating factors that may occur to you, marking the ones you can control with a '*C*' and those you can influence with an '*I*'. These are the areas in which your motivation as a manager can be effective and it could come as a surprise to you to realize just how much you are able to affect the motivation of the people who work for you, not just in the workplace but for twenty-four hours a day, three hundred and sixty-five days a year.

In fact, even on holiday, although your influence may be weakened, it will still be present, while in the workplace itself the way in which you motivate individuals can change their lives for the better or for the worse.

SMILE! YOU'RE MOTIVATING

Smiles are cost-effective and are within the control of every manager.

Make a point of greeting individually all the people who work for you, by name wherever possible and with a smile.

If your staff is small enough, exchange a few words with each of them when you meet them for the first time in the day. If you have a large staff, try to say at least, 'Hi! How are things going?' to a few of them.

MAKE TIME

Set aside a certain time each day for talking to individual members of staff – perhaps after your morning meeting, if you have one.

Make sure everyone knows that your door is open during that time for one-on-one discussions lasting not more than five minutes. If they think they are going to need longer they should make an appointment.

A couple of minutes is often enough for people to put forward suggestions, grumble or ask for a decision. You get the advantage of feedback and contact but, more importantly, the people concerned know that you consider their views are interesting enough to listen to. The advantage, for both you and them, is that – in addition to settling the immediate problem – they will then be able to concentrate on the job in hand for the rest of the day.

The few seconds' contact when you greet people in the morning and the short discussions later on are enough for you to measure the morale of the group. They are also an opportunity for you to encourage and inspire individuals with your confidence and optimism, and to make them feel good about themselves. The ability to do this, especially when things are not going well either for the group or the individual, is the mark of a good leader.

THE OPPORTUNIST MOTIVATOR

Don't miss a chance to motivate individuals in the course of the working day.

Their every contact with you should make them feel enthused, revitalized and reassured about their value to the team. Even if you have to censure somebody, you can do so in a constructive way which leaves them feeling good about you and themselves.

If they seem down, ask them if they have a problem. It could be something you could settle in a couple of minutes or it might be something more serious which you need to talk about in more detail.

'Stroke' wherever possible. Opportunistic stroking can be work-related: 'Great job you did on the Anderson contract, Terry', or as apparently banal as: 'I like the new suit'. Noticing people, especially if it's the boss who is doing the noticing, is motivating.

HORSES FOR COURSES

Avoid monotony and encourage multi-skilling by swapping jobs around occasionally and for short periods but, for the rest of the time, assign tasks to people you know will be good at them and will enjoy them. If you are not certain which jobs appeal to which members of your staff, *ask* them.

Known as 'cafeteria' job assignment, this gives people a motivating control of their own working lives, requires little cash expenditure and is equally effective whether you are managing labourers or lawyers.

Rebecca Jenkins, for example, who runs a nationwide distribution company, finds that drivers fall into two main categories, those who get a kick out of doing a different job every day with new routes and new people, and others who prefer going down the same old road, leaving at the same time, meeting the same people and getting back at the same time. Rebecca explains, 'We try to find out what the drivers want and what they like to do and build the job round them. It doesn't always work, but that is our aim and intention and all the drivers know that.'

Give people who are already well motivated the most challenging jobs they can tackle. For instance, if you need someone to handle a specific job, you could try an approach like: 'Samantha, I'd like you to take over from Mike as Customer Relations Officer. I know you can handle it and both Mike and I will be available to help with any problems you may have at first. If you do as well as I think you will, we could think about a permanent appointment.'

MOTIVATING PEOPLE WITH DULL JOBS

Unfortunately, there are still a great many jobs around which are dull and repetitive, and as a new manager you are more likely to have such tasks to assign than managers of senior grades.

Remember that 'other people are not you' and that there are some who are happy to perform routine jobs. There's an old story about the manager who asked an assembly line worker if he didn't get bored. 'Oh no,' replied the man, 'if things get a bit dull I just move to the other side.'

Move workers who like routine 'to the other side' occasionally, but otherwise leave them to get on with it. On the other hand, you should seek out anyone who is bored or restless and assess their potential for a more interesting job. You could find, for example, that a bored and resentful clerk in the sales office would be great as a member of your outside sales team.

TREAT INDIVIDUALS AS INDIVIDUALS

As well as being different from each other, we are all egocentric, and while we frequently reproach others with remarks like 'You think the whole world revolves around you', we *know* that the world revolves around *us*.

Managers have to accept that the vital question they must answer when dealing with individuals is 'What's in it for me?'.

This is realistic rather than cynical. By listening to what people have to say about *their* hopes and fears you are showing genuine leadership care. By allaying their fears and helping them to realize their hopes and ambitions you are motivating rather than manipulating.

Both hopes and fears can change with age and circumstances, and good managers are able to vary the way they motivate accordingly. The vital thing to remember is that each individual member of the staff must know that they are important to you and the team, that their contribution counts and that they can make a difference to the team's performance.

MOTIVATING BY CHALLENGE

Setting realistic and challenging targets for individual employees is a controllable factor and is extremely motivating.

Targets should be set after consultation with the person concerned who should agree that the task is important and that the targets, though challenging, are reasonable.

This marriage of challenge and involvement doubles the individual's motivation.

Whenever possible, people should be involved in any decision relating to their own work, their training, their careers and even such apparently trivial matters as moving their desk.

REWARDS AND RECOGNITION

As a front-line manager you should be able to control, or at least influence, the tangible rewards on offer to your staff, like pay and bonuses, and these should be fair and equitable, representing a suitable reward for time and energy expended and work done. 'A fair day's wage for a fair day's work' is the aim of every employee, whether don or dustman.

As far as bonuses are concerned, one national newspaper editor we knew used to send notes to reporters who had done a good job, saying, 'We are giving you what our friends in the legal profession call a refresher' and the word is appropriate.

Financial refreshers can be backed up by other rewards which can vary in value according to circumstances. IML, for example, awards small items like pens and mugs for individual contributions in the course of its motivation campaigns.

'Stroking' individuals can be equally effective, especially if the verbal pat on the back is reinforced by an official letter and an item on the staff notice board. Like financial rewards, praise and other forms of recognition have to be justified and fair. It's no use motivating one individual at the expense of demotivating a dozen or so others.

PROMOTION AND PROMISES

Promotion is one way of rewarding individuals which should be in your gift and it could be the most important one.

It is a reward which is, and should be, closely bound up with training and performance and, ironically, one which in the long run could deprive you of your best workers.

This sometimes leads managers to train and promote the people they want to get rid of, while holding back the good performers in order to keep them in the team. Not unnaturally this can lead to resentment: and in the end is demotivating and demoralizing for the people who deserve to be allowed to realize their full potential.

Promotion out of the team may be good for the individual and for the organization but most managers will wish for more immediate benefits for themselves and their team.

On the whole, the best answer to this dilemma is to make individual members of your staff aware that you have a training and promotion policy based on performance. The knowledge that someone who did a good job for you was promoted, even though it meant that you lost them, is more motivating than a promise which circumstances may make it impossible to keep.

Remember that the manager's joke syndrome means that your 'I'll see what I can do' becomes a firm promise and that promises which are not kept – even those which exist only in the mind of the person concerned – have a tremendously demotivating effect.

MEN MOTIVATING WOMEN

As a male manager who wishes to motivate a woman member of his staff, you will be helped rather than otherwise by the fact that the other person is patently 'not you', and will therefore react differently to some motivating factors than you would yourself. Once again, the difference is in the mix rather than the motivation.

The obvious 'difference' will help you to avoid such demotivating factors as sexism, condescension and so on, and encourage you to exercise leadership, charm and charisma.

Don't take women for granted by assuming, for example, that if there is one woman in your team it will always be she who makes the coffee. Avoid anything which could be seen as sexual innuendo. Even women who appear to be enjoying and responding to dubious humour are often unhappy about it. Of course, many women enjoy the occasional *risqué* joke or witticism but you have to know people well before you can be certain of this.

In fact, it is not the odd joke or the off-the-cuff crack that demotivates women to the point of despair but the constant barrage of juvenile smut they experience for eight hours of every working day in many workplaces, especially small offices.

71

One of your important motivating functions is to protect women from this and any other form of harassment and to be sufficiently sensitive to see when a stiff upper lip is trembling.

As always, good manners is the key. If you are thoughtful and courteous to your female employees at all times, especially when dealing with them individually, your words and actions will be the correct and most motivating ones.

WOMEN MOTIVATING MEN

Female managers will find many male employees incredibly sensitive and difficult to motivate – especially to begin with. Of men who have never worked for a woman boss, 42 per cent admit that they would be chary of doing so, but women are filling more and more managerial slots and men will have to get used to it.

Some 20 per cent of women bosses have created the business they manage, while the rest have moved up to management. Only a very few have taken over family businesses or obtained their position by influence. This means that most women managers can motivate male employees by the fact that they got the job on merit and are therefore extremely competent.

Here again, women can use charm to motivate. They should also be quick to involve and even to ask, if indirectly, for help. They should forget aggressiveness and use tact and diplomacy.

In the end, the fact that women managers have to try harder and must be more competent, more sensitive and more tactful than their male counterparts makes them very motivating leaders to work for.

This also applies when women managers have to motivate individual women members of their staff, except that, very often, they need to be even more sensitive, tactful and so on, and avoid imitating the worst of their male colleagues, as women tend to be hard on their more successful sisters.

Remember: 'That's just like a woman!' should be a compliment.

THE CONTROL QUOTIENT

As a front-line manager in daily contact with the people reporting to you, your control quotient in this area should be high. Most of the factors are those over which you can exercise control on your own authority and, if you do not have complete control over the financial rewards offered to your staff, you should be able to influence them.

HOW WILL YOU KNOW YOU HAVE SUCCEEDED?

It's easier to spot a well-motivated individual than it is to define one, but you will know you have succeeded when the improvement in their performance becomes obvious.

As a result of your efforts and understanding, individuals should be more cheerful, more effective, more willing and enthusiastic, more innovative, more loyal to you as leader and better team players.

You will know that you have really succeeded when formerly sullen, lazy and resentful people begin motivating the people round them.

SUMMARY

- Why you need to be aware that the individual members of your staff you need to motivate are 'not you' and will not respond to motivation in exactly the same way. For one thing, he or she will almost certainly *not* be a manager.
- How to use the 'W' questions to decide how to motivate individuals.
- Motivating individuals at a distance for twenty-four hours a day. A simple exercise to determine the surprising number of factors *you* can control or influence.
- Why smiles are 'cost-effective' and why you should be an opportunistic motivator seizing every chance to motivate, as well as making time to see individuals.
- Horses for courses or, how to motivate individuals by 'cafeteria' job assignment.

- Why you should tell people 'what's in it for them'. The importance of rewards and recognition, financial and otherwise.
- Promotions, promises and how to win by putting employees first.
- Men motivating women; women motivating men; and women motivating other women.
- How you will know if you have been successful in motivating individual members of your team.

EIGHT

Motivating Groups

In some ways motivating groups is easier than motivating individuals, partly because it is easier to establish the 'culture' of a group, but also because of the synergy generated by people working together.

We have already seen how this almost magical phenomenon ensures that the effect of two or more people, acting as a team, is greater than the sum of their individual effects and, in fact, there seems to be virtually no limit to what a group can be motivated to attempt.

Sports teams, for example, can be motivated to play and win against seemingly impossible odds; motivation has enabled expeditions to struggle on when all hope seems lost; teams of highly motivated scientists have placed a man on the moon. The power generated within a motivated group can even persuade individuals to sacrifice their lives.

THE POWER OF MOTIVATION

In fact, motivation itself is neither good nor bad, and the same force which, in two world wars, persuaded millions of otherwise ordinary human beings to kill people and to put their own lives at risk, can be adapted to get a relatively small number to do the best work of which they are capable.

One thing which emerges clearly from the ways in which men were persuaded to enlist and to go into battle is how much motivating groups of people differs from motivating individuals.

Imagine a World War I general trying to persuade an individual civilian to take part in the Battle of the Somme.

'Well, Mr Atkins, what we want you to do for your king and

country is perfectly simple. First of all we are going to give you a rifle and transport you to a muddy trench where you will be subjected to a barrage of shellfire. If you survive, we would then like you to leave the shelter of the trench and advance, without protection, into a hail of rifle and machine-gun fire towards a thicket of barbed wire, in an effort to get to grips with a well-trained and well-armed enemy who, if you don't kill him, will most certainly kill you.'

This is a sober version of what the hundreds of thousands of men who went to the Western Front *knew* they would be facing and, while it is easy to imagine Mr Atkins's answer when approached as an individual, millions of Mr Atkinses, Monsieur Duponts and Herr Schmidts went off to near-certain death or injury because the groups of which they were members were motivated to do so.

HOW DID THEY DO IT?

However much we deplore the outcome, motivating millions to face the near certainty of becoming a casualty was an incredible feat, and to pull it off the authorities in the countries concerned used every motivating factor available.

Some of these are not applicable to your situation as a newly promoted manager, mainly because they savour of manipulation rather than motivation, but others can be adapted for use in the workplace.

The more important motivating factors used by the military 'management' included:

- *a noble cause*. The mass of recruits were persuaded that by going to war they would be engaged in a patriotic struggle, in the course of which they would defend the cause of justice;
- *recognition, approbation* and *increased status*. As members of the group, factory hands, clerks and farm boys put on uniform and became 'instant' heroes;
- *comradeship*. The wartime army turned recruits into comrades, prepared to make any sacrifice for their 'band of brothers'. Later, some brilliant but cynical motivator had

the idea of forming 'Pals' Battalions, which led to the menfolk of whole townships enlisting *en masse*;

- *opportunities*. Recruiters could offer genuine 'opportunities for advancement'. Those who lived were virtually certain of promotion;
- *goals and deadlines*. The goal was to beat the enemy and make sure that it was 'all over by Christmas';
- *public relations and propaganda*. Every possible means was used to whip up hatred of the enemy and present the leaders as *visible*, all-knowing, all-powerful, godlike creatures who nevertheless could, on carefully stage-managed occasions, reveal a 'human' side;
- *peer pressure*. Those reluctant to become heroes were pressured by their fellows, their families and certain groups – like the women who handed out white feathers to men not wearing uniform;
- *promises*. Soldiers were promised not only that their jobs would be waiting for them but that they would return to 'a land fit for heroes' – a good example of a motivating catchphrase;
- *discipline*. Group discipline, together with 'drill', was used to inculcate habits of obedience;
- *fitness*. Thanks to group exercises and sports, most of the recruits felt fitter when they went 'over the top' than they had ever been in their lives;
- *fear*. Soldiers were welded together by fear of the enemy, and of their own side who were ready to shoot them for 'cowardice';
- *events*. The war itself was an exciting and motivating *event*;
- *leadership*. Most platoons, companies and regiments were motivated by genuine and, in many cases, inspired leaders who were literally 'front-line' managers.

THE POWER IS WITH YOU

Even as a new manager you will be able to adapt most of the powerful motivating factors listed above to the business of motivating your 'troops' in the workplace.

While you will not need to motivate people to act against their own interests, you will have to persuade them to perform tasks which they would not do if left to their own devices. In fact, one interesting way of determining the function of management is to imagine a group of individuals set down in an office or shop floor without any instructions or guidance. It would be a while before they made any move whatsoever and there would be no guarantee that when they did move it would be in any constructive way.

Your task as manager is to take a bunch of people who, if left to their own devices, would either stand still or move every which way, and to get them to pull together.

A surprising number of the factors used to motivate troops can be used to persuade your staff to do their best work. These include:

A 'NOBLE' CAUSE

This appears to be a tough one for front-line managers to control, but you could find that your organization already has a 'mission' which you can use to enthuse your people. A cause need not be big in order to be noble. Something like persuading your staff to work for a local charity or to protect the environment can build up team spirit and help change 'us and them' into 'we'.

With this sort of noble cause your *Control* factor is high but, while you can make suggestions, the cause should be decided in consultation with staff, and managers and management must be *seen* to be playing their part. If you and your staff decide, for example, to clear up a local waterway, you have to be seen on the site and management should make a gesture by providing tools, transport, refreshments and so on.

RECOGNITION

There are no medals in the workplace, even though they did work in the former Soviet Union for a while, but other forms of recognition have a high *control* factor for the front-line manager.

Public praise for individuals who do a good job is motivating for the group, as it is for teams or for the whole staff.

Don't debase the currency by praising where praise is unwarranted, but don't miss any opportunity to recognize good work, preferably in such a way that the whole organization is aware of it.

Increase the status of successful groups by confirming their identity, if possible by giving them a name and perhaps group ties and scarves or stickpins. Items like distinctive clipboards and 'customized' pens can serve the same purpose.

COMRADESHIP

It's unlikely that you or your staff will be required to face shot and shell but a feeling of comradeship should develop naturally as people realize that they are 'all in the same boat'. Unfortunately it is all too easy for this sort of comradeship to become exclusive and managers need to make it clear that, as 'cox', they are in the same boat as their staff.

As the feeling of comradeship grows, individuals become more ready to help each other and even to make sacrifices for the sake of the group. Direct *control* of this factor is not easy but you can encourage the growth of comradeship by recognizing group loyalties – even if misguided.

OPPORTUNITIES FOR DEVELOPMENT AND ADVANCEMENT

The knowledge that people who perform well will be trained and considered for promotion is highly motivating for the group and this is a factor which you should be able to *control* or at least *influence*.

Use promotion within your department to reward good work and make sure that everyone in your group knows that it is your policy to do this. Team leaders, ecpecially, should know that proving themselves could lead to advancement.

Encourage your people to take advantage of any appropriate training on offer. Keep your boss informed about individuals who show potential and, once again, make sure that everyone knows that this is your policy.

GOALS AND DEADLINES

Group goals are extremely motivating, especially if there is a deadline attached to them, and they should be specific, agreed by the group and attainable, with intermediate goals on the way.

We can remember otherwise cynical reporters taking crazy risks to get news stories and pictures back to base in time to meet deadlines, and managers should be aware that people, especially young people, working in groups where motivation is high, are prone to take risks, even if only by overworking.

PUBLIC RELATIONS

'Public Relations' can refer to your relationship with your staff and the staff of your organization, as well as to the general public. In this sense it has a high *control* factor for front-line managers.

Public relations has to do with the way you are perceived by your 'public' and you should remember that you are playing a role you have been cast to play (i.e. that of front-line manager), you have decided on the way in which you will interpret the role (i.e. your style of management) and that, perhaps most important of all, you are on stage at all times.

Many management theorists assert that managers should have 'humility' in the sense that they should be unpretentious and aware of their failings, but the word has uncomfortable Uriah Heapish connotations. It also evokes the wonderful cartoon in which a wife hisses to her husband who is about to receive an award: 'Remember, darling, you're not big enough to be humble!'

Not many of us are 'big enough to be humble', but one quality managers do need is humanity, and nearly all great leaders have realized that, provided it is not overdone, a touch of humanity – an act of clemency here, a man-to-man chat with the man in the street there, or even a trademark like a corn cob pipe – is excellent public relations.

Managers should be aware of the effect that their words and

actions have on their staff and make sure that they are seen in the best and most motivating light. This element of management is so important that we shall be referring to the mechanics of it under the heading of 'communication'.

PEER PRESSURE

Fear of people thinking badly of us is extremely motivating and has a high *control* factor, but managers who make use of it have to be careful to avoid any suggestion of manipulation.

You might, for instance, point out to a group of employees that absenteeism and persistent lateness is increasing the workload for everyone – and motivate the whole group into becoming unofficial, but extremely effective, time-keepers. Again, by saying that pilfering could lead to the closure of a department you might turn the whole group into security guards.

Obviously, although peer pressure can be used in this way, too much of it savours of the classroom and such threats as, 'If the person responsible does not come forward the whole class will be given an hour's detention'. Treating adults like naughty children is demotivating.

It's far better to use this sort of pressure sparingly and positively to ensure, for example, that the group persuades and helps individual members to realize their potential.

PROMISES

One of the most effective ways of persuading a group of people to do as you wish is to promise them: 'If you do this for me, I will see that you are rewarded', but promises must be kept.

Remember the old saying that you can fool all the people some of the time and some of the people all of the time but you *can't* fool all the people all the time.

Adolf Hitler, for example, achieved miracles of motivation by promising 'Today Germany – tomorrow the whole world', but, as soon as it became obvious that he would not be able to keep his promises, motivation gave place not merely to demotivation but total disenchantment.

81

Promises have a high *control* factor but managers should remember that if they make a firm promise *they* are responsible for its being kept, even if they have been forced to break it by their superiors or events outside their control. Good intentions don't count and, as broken promises are demotivating, there is perhaps a case for the 'definite maybe' or at least an escape clause on the lines of 'God willing'.

DISCIPLINE

Discipline sounds almost out of place in a modern book on management, but the word comes from a Latin word meaning 'to teach', referring especially to the teaching of rules of behaviour.

In this sense managers are 'teachers' whose job is to see that the rules laid down by senior management are followed, and to formulate additional rules of conduct for their staff where necessary.

This is not as difficult as it sounds because most people, especially those who work in groups, like to lead an ordered existence and prefer to know exactly 'how far they can go'.

The best rules of conduct for groups are those established by consensus and imposed by peer pressure. A front-line manager, for example, could suggest that latecomers were holding up the work of the whole department, and that in future everyone arriving late, including themselves, should put a pound in the office charity collection box. Provided the majority agreed, the staff themselves would see that this 'disciplinary' rule was kept.

Making rules for your own convenience like 'In future the parking space in front of the main entrance is reserved for the manager!' is demotivating. Suggesting rules which will improve things for the group is motivating.

FITNESS

Health and fitness are highly motivating for individuals and groups. They are factors which new managers may be able to *control* by advertising in-house or outside fitness programmes, forming departmental sports teams, and by force of example.

New managers, particularly, should keep fit themselves and, where possible, take part in their department's sports activities.

This is not only motivating in itself but also provides useful inter-grade contact for everyone concerned.

Managers should also keep an eye on the general fitness of their staff, watching for safety hazards like dangerous machines or bad lighting and keeping on the look out for signs of stress or illness.

They should also practise damage control by, for example, sending home people with streaming colds before they infect the whole staff.

FEAR

Rule by fear has no place in modern management, although people should be aware that if they consistently fail to do their jobs properly and do not accept and respond to training, or if they persistently break the rules, sanctions will follow. In order to maintain group motivation, everyone should know what will not be tolerated and what the sanctions will be.

However, many employees have an illogical fear of their boss which can be demotivating for the individual concerned and for the group. Managers should try to dispel these fears where they exist.

EVENTS

New managers may not have much *control* over major events within their organization, but they should be able to exert some *influence* on them. They may be required, for instance, to implement senior management initiatives like quality or motivation campaigns.

You should have much more control over minor events like competitions and presentations. These can be motivating, especially for people doing routine jobs, and managers should make the most of them to promote team spirit among their staff.

LEADERSHIP

Inspired, inspiring and visible leadership is highly motivating in the workplace and is something over which you should have a great deal of *control*. It includes factors like visibility – Management by Walking About – your frankness and the way in which you care for and back up your staff.

Good managers not only administer justice fairly, but actively seek justice for their team, even if this means risking the displeasure of their own superiors.

Real leadership means responsibility for all the team's activities – failures as well as successes. Only if you accept this and are known to be prepared to back your people at all times can you expect to inspire *loyalty* – the real bonus for any manager who is also a leader.

'SNAFU' – AND HOW TO AVOID IT

One of the things which most demotivates groups is the feeling that they are being 'messed about'.

This state of affairs, which the American Army once described as SNAFU or 'Situation Normal – All Fouled Up', meant that troops were sent to the wrong place, issued with the wrong clothing or weapons and were even sacrificed unnecessarily by superiors who patently thought their men were expendable and didn't give a damn what happened to them.

SNAFU translates into civilian workplaces in terms of meetings arranged and cancelled, unkept appointments, groups of people left waiting by managers who fail to apologize and so on. It can be avoided by good manners and efficient planning.

A JOB WELL DONE

For groups, as for individuals, the satisfaction of a job well done is highly motivating, which accounts for the success of the 'quality' campaigns run by many successful organizations. In this context 'quality' means 'appropriate', rather than 'luxurious', and is closely linked to the ideas of service which we shall be looking at when we consider the 'customers' of front-line managers and their staffs.

THE CONTROL QUOTIENT

Your *control* quotient for the motivation of your group should be high and most decisions will be taken on your own authority. Establish a *control* quotient by quantifying the factors on a scale of one to ten according to how much control you really exercise, and then dividing by the number of factors.

For front-line managers the *control* quotient of all three types of motivation – personal, individual and group – is high, and its cost is minimal in relation to its effectiveness. People like to feel motivated and – once you have overcome any initial inertia – motivation snowballs into an unstoppable force.

HOW WILL YOU KNOW YOU HAVE SUCCEEDED?

There's no mistaking the 'buzz' of excitement which marks a well-motivated department in which people are working hard because they are having fun and absenteeism is low because people enjoy coming to work. Mind you, it is often more difficult to achieve this with a team of filing clerks than a team of film-makers but, whatever your group, it *can* be done and you'll know when you get there.

Meanwhile, you can establish a motivation audit for your team and check progress at intervals in the same way as for a personal motivation audit.

SUMMARY

- The power of group motivation and the need to harness it.
- Motivating sacrifice and how you can adapt the same methods to motivate your staff to do a good job.
- The key factors of group motivation.
- How to use the key factors of group motivation in the workplace.
- The power is with *you*, and should be used with care.

- SNAFU – the demotivation of groups who feel they have been messed about, used, taken for granted and manipulated – and how you can avoid this by sound planning, respect and good manners.
- How motivation 'snowballs'.
- How will you know when you have succeeded in motivating your people? See the quality – sense the 'buzz'!

NINE

Delegating to Individuals

Delegation can change a one-man band into a great orchestra and enable leaders to multiply their efforts hundreds or thousands of times over.

In the workplace it can turn a tiny business into a billion pound conglomerate, so it is little wonder that many successful managers spend 40 per cent or more of their time on delegating.

As a front-line manager you are living proof of the need for delegation in any but the smallest of organizations, as you are almost certainly the final link in a delegating chain which begins with your chief executive.

Obviously, it would be impossible for CEOs to do all the work involved in running large organizations, so they must find a way of getting other people to perform many of the tasks.

One thing chief executives might do, once they realize that they can't do everything themselves, would be to share out the tasks to a number of individuals, laying down detailed rules for their day-to-day working and emergency plans to cover some of the difficulties that might arise. This system, or something very much like it, was operated by many early entrepreneurs and, until recently, by almost all armies. However, there are several drawbacks to this style of leadership, not the least of which is that leaders, like the rest of us, are mortal.

WHY LEADERS MUST DELEGATE

Apart from the consideration that the CEO might move on, retire, or be called to the Great Executive Suite in the Sky, the drawbacks of one person trying to 'run the show' without delegating include the fact that:

- such an organization lacks flexibility as no one but the leader is allowed to make decisions. This makes day-to-day working difficult and renders it impossible to cope adequately with a sudden crisis;
- it is virtually impossible for one person to supervise every detail involved in administering a large group and totally impossible for one leader to take care of all the other functions of management;
- leaders who try to manage simply by cascading tasks to the front line find it difficult to make their organization a team and lose all the benefits of synergy;
- the individuals who are charged with passing on the orders of the CEO to the stage below them would lack motivation;
- there would be no feedback from middle and front-line management, no new ideas, no personal initiatives of any kind;
- the only executives below the CEO would be 'Jobsworths' whose ideas of management would be encapsulated in reactions like 'It's more than my job's worth', 'We've always done things that way', 'It can't be done' and 'I was only carrying out orders'.

WHY SOME MANAGERS HATE TO DELEGATE

An organization of any size in which the CEO failed to delegate at all would soon go out of business, but you may have come across companies in which not only top management but the management as a whole were reluctant to delegate. You may even have worked for such an organization, in which case you will have experienced the difficulties at first hand. You will know how essential it is to delegate and will have asked yourself why people are reluctant to do so.

You may think it is because they hate the thought of giving up even a fraction of their control, but, while some people do like to be autocrats, this is rarely the whole story.

Some people refuse to delegate because they feel, often with some justification, that no one is as capable of doing the jobs which need to be done as they are themselves.

Another, and even more potent reason, is that the leader is accountable for the whole organization and is responsible for other people's mistakes. This means that delegation involves taking risks. Leaders could find, for example, that they had delegated to the wrong person who was either unable to do the job or, worse still, did it so well as to become a threat.

The risks of delegation are real, but they are calculated risks and the advantages of delegating are so great that no manager can afford to ignore them.

MOTIVE, MEANS AND OPPORTUNITY

The risks arise because delegation is vastly different from merely handing out jobs.

Chief executive officers delegate by appointing a number of senior managers who report to them and who are responsible for the work of the people – perhaps junior managers like you – who make up their teams.

In order to do this, the CEOs will have officially delegated some of their authority to their senior managers.

They need to do this because it is no use motivating people to take on a job, and giving them the opportunity to do it, unless you also give them the means to carry out the task – including the necessary authority.

Many managers, whatever their grade, are reluctant to 'share' their authority in this way because they see authority as a finite resource which is lost as soon as it is given to someone else. Some junior managers feel this more than their senior colleagues because they have less authority to begin with.

Fortunately, authority is not something which leaders have to take away from themselves in order to give to someone else, but is like a cellular structure which divides in order to grow, in much the same way that human cells divide, grow and specialize to form an efficiently functioning body.

DELEGATION IS INVESTING

Delegated authority is 'vested' in the person concerned. It does not detract from the authority of the leader any more than a parson who marries people 'by virtue of the power vested in me' reduces the authority of the bishop or of the Church.

Looked at in this way delegation is an 'in-vestment', which, like all investment, has an element of risk, but one on which the returns can be extremely high.

The investment includes not only authority but, in most cases, time and patience. It should not be made lightly, whatever the potential advantages.

DELEGATION AND THE FRONT-LINE MANAGER

Delegation looks as though it could well be the prerogative of senior managers, as front-line managers have no managers reporting to *them* and therefore appear to be at the end of the delegating chain. In fact, delegation is an important function of front-line management and everything we have said about your chief executive's need to delegate is applicable to *your* situation as a new manager.

You can't do every job of your department yourself, even if you consider that none of your staff is capable of doing the jobs as well as you.

You need to delegate, which means 'investing' some of your authority, in spite of the element of risk, because the potential advantages are so great. They include the fact that delegation:

- gives you more time for your own work and enables you to concentrate on the things you do best, the things you were appointed to do and which require your individual skills and experience;
- prevents you from being bogged down by routine;
- makes you a 'pro-active' manager by freeing you to plan for the future, to anticipate and initiate, rather than merely reacting;
- motivates the individuals you select. Don't forget that some tasks which you now find routine and boring will be as fresh

and exciting to them as they were to you when you first
tackled them;

- often reveals that other people can do the job better and
  more quickly than you can;
- trains people to accept and handle responsibility. This should
  mean that you have a pool of people who are ready and
  willing to help you seize any opportunities which may arise.
  You should also have at least one person who could take
  over the running of your department while you are ill or on
  holiday (*see next chapter*);
- provides you with satisfactions. Grooming people by
  delegating is highly satisfying. If the people you are
  managing realize their full potential, you become bigger and
  your authority increases rather than diminishes.

THE DIFFICULTIES OF DELEGATION – AND HOW TO OVERCOME THEM

The main drawback in delegating tasks to subordinates is the
possibility that they may not be able to do the job or that they
will make a mess of it.

This possibility exists, but the risk is a calculated one. You
should not invest blindly in a subordinate, any more than you
would invest in a company without being well informed about
its character, its track record and its potential. As a new manager,
you should be on the look-out for people to 'invest' in, from the
moment you take over.

However, no matter how good you are, you are bound to make
some mistakes in your judgement of people and their capabilities,
and although it is something which can be learned, it is rare even
for experienced managers to get 'people' judgements right every
time.

Reduce the possibility of error by close observation, but once
you have made your choice give your subordinate the authority
to do the job and the time to make mistakes.

Use motor management (the simplified PACA PACA
sequence) and at all other times, apart from being available in
dire emergencies, practise 'hands-off' management. Trusting

people to do the job and showing them that you believe in their abilities is a major part of their reward for doing it.

A second major drawback of delegation is that delegating a task to someone else frequently means that it takes much longer than doing it yourself. Be patient! Maybe you were not always quite so quick as you are now. Besides, delegation, in this respect, is rather like learning to use a word processor, or studying shorthand. The time it takes pays huge dividends in the end.

Some psychologists believe that the secret fear that people will do the job better than we can is what really prevents many of us from delegating as much as we need to. This is like trying to hold back a younger brother or sister because we fear they will overtake us.

In the case of subordinates there is every chance that they will end up becoming better than you at the task you delegate to them because (1) they have a chance to specialize, (2) they have a different approach, (3) they have the advantage of your guidance and experience and (4) beating you is a challenge.

SOME MORE EXCUSES

Other excuses, valid and otherwise, which managers and especially new managers use for not delegating, or for delegating inadequately, include:

- 'My people aren't mature enough, they haven't the experience.' *Give them some!*
- 'Why should I give responsibility to other people? I'm the one who has to carry the can if things go wrong.' *True – but who gets the lion's share of the credit when things go right?*
- 'I'm a workaholic. I enjoy being under pressure so there's no need for me to delegate.' *Keep up your health insurance subscription!*
- 'If I delegate, there won't be anything left for me to do.' *Ha!*
- 'I can't delegate in case my boss finds out.' *Keep your boss informed!*
- 'I don't like to delegate completely, so I delegate part of a job or delegate the same job to a couple of people to keep

things competitive. Mind you, I do delegate the really nothing jobs to the youngest members of my staff. *How would you like it if your boss behaved like that to you – splitting your authority and depriving you of anything that might be interesting or challenging?*

DELEGATE PEOPLE TO KEEP THEM – EVEN IF ONLY TO KEEP THEM ON YOUR SIDE

If you persistently refuse to delegate tasks to individuals who are capable of doing them, you run the risk of the people concerned becoming sullen and resentful. You also run the more serious risk of losing your best employees. The ideal situation is that they stay with you until you move up and then move up with you. However, if they do leave you, and overtake you, it is better to have them on your side. For one thing, helping people is satisfying and, for another, having as your CEO the person you kept back by refusing to delegate might make life difficult, to say the least.

Think of delegation not in terms of fragmentation but as a preliminary exercise in empire-building.

WHAT NOT TO DELEGATE

There are some things you should *not* delegate, including:

1. The disciplining of someone of equal rank to the person concerned.
2. Anything which involves confidential information restricted to your level of seniority.
3. Work you want to get rid of because you don't like it.
4. Tasks that are patently beyond the skill and competence of the person concerned.

HOW TO DELEGATE IN PRACTICE

Before going on to 'h' for 'how?', check that you have answered, or will be able to answer, all the 'W' questions relevant to the particular piece of delegation: Who? What? Why? Where? When? Then use the PACA PACA sequence.

PACA PACA (1) PLAN

Decide which tasks you wish to delegate, how you are going to delegate and to whom. Your *control* factor is high. You need to be very clear in your own mind as to what you want the person to do.

You need to think about each of the individual members of your team and ask yourself:

1. What skills, qualifications and experience do they have which are not being used to the full? Go back to the CVs if you need to. It is not unusual for managers who have delegated a specialized job to someone from outside to say something like, 'But Tom, I didn't know you spoke Swedish'.
2. What sort of work could they do well, either immediately or with training? What sort of work could they *not* do, even if given training?

PACA PACA (2) ACT

1. You may have to 'sell' the person concerned on the idea of accepting delegated tasks. Explain to him or her that you are relieving them of some less important work, express your faith in their ability, tell them where applicable that the new task could be permanent and carry a title – and more money. *Motivate them*!
2. Explain exactly what you want your subordinate to do. Be patient. Go over things a couple of times and ask questions until you are certain everything is understood.
3. Tell them why you need them to do the job.
4. Show them how to do it. Do *not* demonstrate that *you* can do the job in two seconds flat, while making a 'phone call and drinking a cup of tea.
5. Make sure they have all the information they need to do the

job, or know where to get it, and introduce them to any people they will be dealing with, whatever their grade.

6. Discuss and settle on a schedule, where applicable, for each stage of the job and set a date for completion.

7. You've given the person concerned the *opportunity* and provided them with suitable *motives*. Make absolutely certain that you also give them the *means*. These may include materials, a budget and assistance, but *must* include the authority needed to get the job done. The person concerned must know they have the authority and any other people concerned, of whatever rank, must be aware of it too.

PACA PACA (3) CONTROL

1. Ask the person to whom you have delegated a job to provide you with regular reports at each stage. Go through the reports with them to make certain that they accord with the facts. Point out, tactfully, if this is not the case, that you need *all* the information, bad news as well as good news, if you are to help where needed.

2. Provide feedback. Stress that you are not annoyed, and will not be annoyed, by mistakes, provided you are told about them. Ask yourself if any mistakes your subordinate may have made were the result of your inadequate planning, poor briefing, etc.

3. Did your subordinate demonstrate lack of confidence or abuse their new authority? If so, they almost certainly need further coaching.

4. Spot check. Supervise the quality of work in progress. Enter, do not invade, your employee's 'territory'. You have a right to be there but you are still a guest, offering help and guidance. Give advice and encouragement in public. Criticize in private.

PACA PACA (4) ACT

1. Evaluate the employee's overall performance, with the person concerned.

2. Reward, praise and encourage good performance – even a good try.
3. Fine-tune the operation at each stage.
4. Provide further coaching where needed, and even if not. Stress your confidence in the person concerned but coach anyway to avoid them feeling isolated.

HANDS-OFF MANAGEMENT

Repeat the PACA PACA sequence as often as necessary but, as soon as things are running smoothly, pull out and let the person you delegated get on with the job. Sometimes known as 'management by exception', this means that apart from being happy to listen to major success stories you *only* want to hear about total disasters. For the rest, no news really is good news and this is what delegation is all about.

THE CONTROL QUOTIENT

Most aspects of delegating to individuals are well within your *control* and you can build in any further controls you need – like reports – at any stage. The expense involved in delegating to individuals is not usually very large, and for most front-line managers it is an essential exercise with a very high *control* quotient.

HOW WILL YOU KNOW YOU HAVE SUCCEEDED?

You will know that you have delegated jobs to individuals successfully when:

- your subordinates find great new ways of doing the tasks you assign to them, some so good you can use them, with suitable acknowledgements, in other delegated tasks;
- you find yourself delegating more;
- other members of your staff are clamouring for delegated tasks;

- your departmental deadlines and targets are met, production and quality improved;
- you have time to plan the work of your department;
- you have the time to take a few days off;
- you *do* take a few days off, *confident* that everything will run smoothly in your absence and that, even if you leave a 'phone number, it is highly unlikely that anyone will ring.

SUMMARY

- Why leaders need to delegate. The choice is between delegation and stagnation.
- Why some managers are reluctant to delegate.
- Delegation as an investment. The risks and the profits.
- Why not only senior managers, but also front-line managers, need to delegate to members of their staff. Why be a one-man band when you can conduct an orchestra?
- The drawbacks of delegation and how to avoid them.
- Some more excuses for not delegating, and why you should not let them affect your decision to do so.
- What *not* to delegate.
- Delegation in practice. Using the PACA PACA sequence and when to change to 'hands-off' management.
- The high *control* quotient of delegation.
- How you will know when you have delegated successfully.

TEN

Delegating to Groups

Delegating to individuals can turn small businesses into larger businesses and increase the productivity of front-line departments.

Delegating to *groups* can turn large businesses into multi-million pound international conglomerates and limping departments into corporate power houses.

As a front-line manager you need to be able to delegate both to individuals and groups if you are to derive the maximum advantage from your department's most important resource – people.

Delegating to groups provides leaders with a number of semi-autonomous teams which greatly increase the leaders' effectiveness and make it possible for their organization to grow.

Where necessary, the groups can be task-specific, so that a company, for instance, can be divided into departments like Production, Sales and so on, with all the benefits specialization entails.

At the same time the groups, if well motivated, develop synergy, turning them into dynamic entities, often capable of immense productivity and with a phenomenal capacity for expansion.

DELEGATION ISN'T ABDICATION

Of course leaders do not abdicate their authority when they set up departments and delegate their operation to teams. They retain control and increase their overall authority by appointing team leaders who report to them.

You can see how this works in practice by observing your

own chief executive officer and their relationship with the senior managers who report to them, and the junior managers – including yourself. Obviously this is a chain of command, a hierarchy of team leaders, each responsible to the manager above them for the successful operation of their team.

You will have noticed that this does *not* involve any diminuition of your CEO's authority. In fact, as your boss and probably your boss's boss report to the chief executive, he or she appears to have near god-like authority.

YOUR DEPARTMENT AS A MINI-COMPANY

Even more than delegating to individuals, delegating to groups seems as though it could be exclusively the business of senior management. After all, as a front-line manager you are lowest on the totem pole with no managers reporting to you, while the senior managers have a pool of trained managers to choose from whenever they need a team leader. All they have to do is to pick the right person for the job.

In fact, although you may have no official managers to choose from, the most important part of your delegating effort will be to pick the right people for the job of team leader, and since they have no managerial titles or signs on their doors to indicate that they are leaders, you also have to find them.

Some front-line managers are the creators or owners of small businesses who for part of the time also act as CEOs and senior management. It is sometimes useful to see yourself as the boss of a small business whose autonomy is limited by the requirements of customers.

We will be returning to this concept but for the moment it is enough to remember that in many respects, one of which is the need to delegate to groups, your problems are those of the CEO 'writ small'.

WORKING WITH TEAMS AND DELEGATING TO TEAMS

We have already discussed the creation of teams and team working but there is a difference – an important one – between creating teams and delegating to teams.

Ordinary workplace teams are groups of people, selected by you and led either by you or by a team leader selected by you, and working in close association with you. Properly motivated by you, or your clone, they can work well and develop synergy, but because they have little or no autonomy the dynamism can fizzle out.

One way of improving the motivation of such teams is to slacken the reins and to let team members have a little control over the way the team works, but although this is a step in the right direction, it is a timid approach which will not lead to dynamism and growth.

By creating a team and assigning a task you have given team members an *opportunity*, and by your efforts as a coach you have *motivated* them. What you now need to do, in order to delegate the task to them, is to give them the *means* to do the job – including the authority. In other words, if you delegate to a team it needs to be *empowered*.

EMPOWERMENT

Empowerment involves allowing front-line operatives, either as individuals or teams, to make 'non-routine' decisions that do not jeopardize the structure of the organization.

Your job, as front-line manager, is to train employees, to form teams, and give team members the confidence to make these 'non-routine' decisions, as well as giving them the power to do so.

Today, the trend is towards 'flatter' organizations with fewer levels of management and more empowerment, but how much you are able to empower, and how soon, depends to a great extent on the 'who' you have in your group, and to you as a new manager your group may not seem to be the brightest and best. In fact, they may well look like 'Theory X' people.

THEORY X AND THEORY Y

American psychologist Douglas McGregor in a book called *The Human Side of Enterprise* suggested two theories about the nature of employees.

Theory X assumed that most people are lazy, shiftless, incapable of taking responsibility and will not work unless motivated by the most basic factors like money or fear.

Theory Y, on the other hand, assumed that most employees have a psychological need to work and that, as adult human beings, they have great potential and will actively strive for achievement and seek out responsibility.

In fact, we all have both Theory X and Theory Y characteristics but the mix varies, both in individuals and groups, and you will find it more difficult to delegate if the workforce you take over leans heavily towards Theory X.

However, unless you find yourself in charge of a bunch of grunting Neanderthals, it is unlikely that your staff will be completely Theory X and you will be able, with patience, to coach them into becoming Theory Y people. You may find that many of them were really Theory Y people all along and were only waiting for a touch of managerial magic – perhaps something as simple as being treated like adults – to wake them from their lethargy. This means that if you are not already managing a group of bright, mustard-keen Theory Ys, your best bet is to increase their confidence by training and encouragement and by forming them into well-composed teams with a good team leader.

Above all, you must allay the fear that bedevils many employees, namely that if they take a decision, either individually or as a team, which turns out to be a mistake, they will be blamed.

Point out that you are asking for their help in making the decision in question but that *you* are responsible, whatever the outcome. At the same time, you should minimize the risk by *not* empowering people to make big decisions until they are ready to do so.

SELECTING A LEADER FOR A DELEGATED TEAM

Selecting a leader for a team you intend to empower is different from the selection of individual employees for individual tasks within your group.

For example, if as a sales manager you were selecting an individual from your group to introduce a specific line in a particular territory, your choice would be governed by things like the person's product knowledge, qualifications and track record.

Appointing a sales person is a good example of delegating a task to an individual and empowering them to carry it out because, as the name implies, a sales representative is a person delegated to *represent* the company.

Supposing, however, that you wanted to appoint a sales supervisor to lead a team of salespeople.

The individual concerned would not need to be a star performer, although they would have to have done the job and done it well. In fact, a sales superstar might be entirely the wrong person for the job. The ideal team leader should have managerial qualities and potential, in addition to which they should want to take on the responsibility involved and be anxious to succeed.

If you are fortunate, you will have one or more people like this on your staff. If not, you will have to hire them or pick someone who seems to have the spark, and coach them, by empowering them to carry out individual tasks and then putting them in charge of small *ad hoc* teams until they are ready to become team leaders.

DRAWBACKS AND EXCUSES

Many managers exaggerate the drawbacks of delegating to teams led by members of their staff, in much the same way as they do the drawbacks of delegating to individuals, and find as many excuses.

Most of these excuses are the same, too, and, in fact, some of the drawbacks are equally real. If for example you delegate someone to lead a team which has a specific task, there is a good chance that the job will take longer than if you led the team yourself.

However, there are two main reasons why managers are reluctant to delegate to team leaders: (1) they fear that the task will not be done well and that they themselves will be blamed; and (2) they have a deep-seated fear that the person they appoint as team leader will turn out to be a management superstar. 'If I put Samantha in charge of a team,' they argue, 'she could be giving *me* orders within the year.'

The first fear is valid but your *control* factor is high. You have picked the team and the team leader and your coaching should enable them to do the job fast and well. It is a calculated risk. The second fear may also be valid but here your *control* factor is low.

If you are a high-flier to whom Samantha feels loyal she may be content to move up as you do. If not, like Fred, to whom you delegated an individual task, she is quite likely to overtake you.

The difference is that, while Fred will probably become a senior specialist of some sort, Samantha – who you picked because she was efficient and a bit bossy in a friendly sort of way – could finish up running the company.

Hold back the Samanthas of this world and you are going to make them resentful – perhaps even revengeful.

Encourage them and you could finish up with:

- a super-leader to manage your teams for as long as they stay with you;
- the credit for having identified and brought on potential super-managers, which will stand you in good stead with your company and with the people who work for you;
- friends at court, whether as bosses or allies.

PLAN TO KEEP CONTROL

It may well seem that in delegating to a team leader you are working without a net but the *control* factor may be higher than you think.

For one thing, using the PACA PACA sequence, you get to

pick the team leader, to assign the task and to lay down the ground rules.

More importantly, by the time you reach the second planning stage, you should be ready, if need be, to implement an alternative plan which could involve replacing an unsatisfactory team leader or scrapping the team and starting from scratch.

THE WORST POSSIBLE SITUATION SCENARIO

Delegation is one of the many cases where you should make use of the '*worst possible situation scenario*', which simply means that, while confidently expecting the best, you should actively prepare for the worst.

Ask yourself, 'What is the worst thing that could possibly happen?' In this case your delegated team leader could go mad, make a complete mess of the job you have entrusted to them and offend everyone concerned, including not only the members of the team but also people outside your group, including some of your fellow-managers.

Obviously, you need a fall-back plan, in this instance probably a fall-back person and an alternative way of getting the job done.

The worst possible situation scenario will enable you to plan for catastrophe, which means that handling minor hiccups will be easy. Perhaps more importantly, it can expose weaknesses in your original plan. Did you, for instance, give the leader a more important team task to carry out than they could handle? Did you forget to inform the managers of other departments *in writing* that you had appointed a named member of your staff to be team leader, with clearly defined tasks and authority?

SELECTING DELEGATED TEAMS

If you are really going to delegate to teams and empower them, you need to select your team as well as your team leader with even more care than if you were selecting people to work in a closely supervised team.

In addition to *team-building*, which entails filling each 'role' in the team to make sure you have the right mix of qualifications and temperaments, you also have to ensure as far as possible that your team members are compatible with each other and with their leader.

Will they 'get on' and work together? Have they worked together successfully in the past?

One additional thing to watch for is team members who 'get on' *too* well. Some managers have a list of staff members who they will not put into the same team because, although fine when working individually or with others, once they get together they behave like irresponsible clowns.

USING DELEGATED TEAMS

Delegated teams can be used to carry out all the tasks for which supervised teams are used and you can turn supervised teams into empowered teams as a gradual process.

It's up to you to decide, given your knowledge of your staff and their evolution in the direction of Theory Y, whether to let your people test the water of delegation or to throw them in at the deep end.

Delegated teams can handle specific tasks, identify and solve problems, and brainstorm ideas just as supervised teams do. The advantage however is that, once they are off and running, you can leave delegated teams to get on with things, which means you can spend more time doing jobs at *your* optimum performance level – like motivating and delegating. In other words, delegation gives leaders more time to lead.

DELEGATING YOUR MANAGERIAL INITIATIVES

Provided you take over a Theory Y group, or are able to coach your staff to adopt Theory Y attitudes, delegating to groups is an ideal way of handling managerial initiatives, both your own and those of senior management.

You could, for example, come up with a 'brilliant' idea which could improve the performance of every member of your staff. However, to introduce radical changes throughout your department would involve a great deal of upheaval, an unwarranted investment in time and money, especially if the idea turned out to be less brilliant in practice than you imagined.

Forming a delegated team to do the job and empowering them to make it work could be the answer.

That way you give the team a challenging problem and limit the consequences of any possible error – all of which makes it an easier 'package' to sell to your boss than a plan to change the whole of your organization overnight.

DELEGATION AND QUALITY CIRCLES

One example of how delegation might be used to implement a senior management initiative would be total quality control which 'cascades' from the CEO's office to the front line.

Setting up quality circles might be a requirement, but you would soon realize that if you were to try to organize the whole thing yourself you would have little time for anything else.

The National Society for Quality Circles provides the answer in its official definition of quality circles as 'A small group of between three and twelve people who do the same or similar work, voluntarily meeting together for about an hour a week in paid time, usually under the leadership of their own supervisor, and trained to identify, analyse and solve some of the problems in their work, presenting solutions to management and where possible implementing the solutions themselves.'

Appointing the coach, training the team to use the PACA PACA sequence and increasing the number of solutions the team are able to implement themselves is an effective use of delegation. It also emphasizes management's recognition of the fact that the people who know most about a job and how to improve it are the people who do it.

DELEGATION AND SELF-DIRECTED TEAMS

Another senior management initiative you might be required to implement is the setting up of self-managed or self-directed teams, which is a move towards the ultimate in delegation.

A self-directed work team is a group of about eight to twelve people who are empowered to manage every aspect of the job they do – on a day-to-day basis.

This means that the teams, which are a permanent part of the organizational structure, have their own budgets, and the authority to work out how best to do the job. To do this they plan the job, schedule it, make decisions about production problems and are often authorized to recruit new members of the team.

Self-directed teams motivate employees to become Theory Y people by enabling them to become 'thinkers' as well as 'workers' and encourage multi-skilling as team members coach each other to tackle most or all of the team's tasks.

DELEGATION AND INVOLVEMENT

Delegation to self-directed teams means that the team members '*own*' not just a single process or problem but their whole section of the department's task and are responsible for its success or failure.

Such teams virtually run their own 'business' within the department. This is involvement of a very high order and, while highly motivating in itself, should also be suitably rewarded. Such rewards can be in the form of bonuses geared to the team's performance which you should be able to control or influence, or participation schemes over which you may have very little influence.

If no financial reward is built into the structure your only recourse is to motivate by, for example, giving teams names and team leaders titles and by emphasizing the advantages in terms of 'higher' factors like esteem and self-actualization. You should also point out their ultimate financial dependence on the company's growth and success. At the same time, especially if the team is successful, you should push your senior management to provide financial rewards.

Involvement changes 'us and them' into 'we', but when times are difficult some organizations revert to 'stick' as opposed to 'carrot' management, while others are able to persuade their workforce that everyone in the company has a stake in it. Do your best to increase involvement in your department – your survival and theirs could depend on it.

DELEGATION AND THE CUSTOMER

Delegation in all its phases, but especially as you move towards self-directed teams, means that front-line workers are increasingly required to deal with customers both internal and external and are responsible for the quality of the service they give to them.

Your job as a front-line manager is to facilitate the dealings of your team with customers, to enable them and empower them to make decisions affecting customers and to coach them towards continuous improvement of the product or service they provide.

THE CONTROL QUOTIENT

The amount of *control* front-line managers are able to exercise over delegated teams is higher than would at first appear. As front-line manager you are responsible for setting up both the teams and the framework in which they will operate, for coaching them, for assessing their progress and supervising their activities on a regular basis. You are also the one who controls or influences the team's rewards, tangible and otherwise.

HOW WILL YOU KNOW YOU HAVE SUCCEEDED?

You will know that you have delegated successfully if your people are utilizing all their skills and creative talents to further the aims of the organization and are happy with their work and their prospects.

Signs that things are going well will include better interpersonal relations, better quality of production and better service to customers, a reduction in absenteeism and in unpunctuality, together with a decline in petty dishonesty.

Importantly to you, because of the possible effect on your own career, the results of your delegation, especially delegation to teams, are quantifiable. Delegation usually leads to decreases in waste and increases in production which have a dramatic effect on your department's bottom line.

You should also find that you have saved yourself *time* – a resource so important that we have devoted a whole section to its management.

SUMMARY

- How delegation can turn your teams into dynamic entities capable of continuous self-improvement.
- Why delegating to your teams doesn't mean that you abdicate *control*, any more than your chief executive officer does when he delegates to you and your department.
- Empowerment – allowing front-line employees to make 'non-routine' decisions.
- Excuses for not delegating to groups and why you should not allow them to prevent you from delegating to your teams.
- Introducing the 'worst possible situation scenario'.
- How to select and delegate teams to implement your own initiatives and those of senior management. Delegation and quality circles.
- Progressing towards self-directed teams and the continuing role of the front-line manager.

PART THREE

Time Management

ELEVEN

Time to Manage

If you are not managing your working time properly you are 'cheating' your company – unintentionally of course – by not giving it what it has paid for.

This is because time is a finite resource for all organizations and a valuable one in which they invest a great deal of money – an investment on which they are entitled to expect a reasonable return.

The 'cheating' arises because employers place a value on people's time based on the return they can expect from it and, as they expect more from their managers' time than that of their front-line employees, they are prepared to pay more for it.

The sums are simple:

- if you are being paid £40,000 a year and your secretary's salary is £20,000, any work *you* do which could be done by your secretary is costing your company money at the rate of around an extra £10 an hour;
- if you waste your own working time by frittering it away you are costing your company £20 an hour;
- if you allow your staff to waste time, which they too have sold to the company, you are costing the company around £10 per hour or more per person;
- if you misuse your time or allow your staff to misuse theirs you could estimate a loss of £10 an hour for yourself and £5 an hour for each member of your staff.

TIME IS REAL MONEY

Before you decide that the above amounts are small potatoes compared with your department's overall budget, it's worth considering how much of that budget goes on buying people's time – i.e. on salaries and wages.

How much of this time is wasted? American expert Dr De Woot claims that executives who have not been trained in time management spend 49 per cent of their time on work which could be done by their secretaries, and 47 per cent of their time on work which should have been delegated to other people.

This means that they are spending only 4 per cent of their energy on tasks that utilize to the full the abilities and talents for which the company is paying them and that the company is not getting full value for 97 per cent of their salaries and overhead costs.

TIME AND THE FRONT-LINE MANAGER

Obviously a company with '4 per cent managers' is getting no value for the time that managers waste and only around half value for time they misuse, to say nothing of the time their staff waste or misuse. There is tremendous scope for improvement and a genuine managerial challenge.

Fortunately, time management makes it possible to improve this situation dramatically and cheaply. This makes it an ideal initiative for front-line managers whose control of their own working time and that of their staff is almost total.

Like motivation – the other 'magic wand' of front-line management – time management can work miracles if you have the patience to learn how to use it.

Using time management, you will no longer find that you have to work so hard that you have 'no time to manage'.

Instead of regarding time as 'the enemy', you will make time your friend by working smarter rather than harder.

Eventually, time management could double the productivity of your department, but you will find it difficult to coach other people to manage their time if you can't manage your own.

HOW MUCH IS YOUR TIME WORTH?

If you are not convinced that some people's time is worth more than others', remember the old story of the craftsman who was called in to repair a faulty boiler. He looked it over, crawled inside it and struck it one mighty blow with his hammer, after which it worked perfectly. However, when the factory owner got a bill for £100 he was furious: 'But you were only in the factory a couple of minutes, and all you did was to hit the boiler with your hammer'.

'That's all right,' said the craftsman. 'I'll give you another bill', and he wrote out an account reading: 'To examining boiler ... £1. To hitting boiler with hammer ... £1. To knowing where to hit ... £98.'

How much is your working time worth? To you it's worth what you can get for it in terms of salary and benefits, but if you are making a total of, say, £30,000, your company is paying much more than that for your time.

Add on to your salary and benefits the amounts the company pays out in social security contributions, pension, medical and other insurances. Then add your office and its furnishings, office equipment like computers, 'phones and so on, plus lighting, heating and rates. Don't forget your expenses, including your company car if you have one, training seminars and conferences.

If you spend a lot of time out of your office you could cost more to run than you do to hire but, even without a big expense account, you are costing your company at least £1,000 a week, £200 a day or £25 an hour. If you are wasting any time at all, you are wasting more than you think.

HOW MUCH CAN YOU SAVE?

On the basis of £25 an hour, you can work out the cost to your company of: a useless ten-minute phone call; the file it took you a quarter of an hour to find; the time you spent doing jobs other people should have been doing.

At the same rate, a fifteen-minute coffee break costs your company more than a fiver – not counting the coffee.

However, there is no need to become paranoid. Time-misers are almost as bad as time-wasters and, besides, there is usually so much scope for improvement that your time management effort will begin to show results in terms of reduced costs and increased production right from the start.

Don't forget that any of your time that you do *save* will save the company £25 an hour and that, once you have learned to manage your own time, you can coach your staff to save time worth around £10 an hour, multiplied by the number of your staff, which could add up to a lot of money.

Some experts claim that anyone who manages time effectively will save around two hours a day, but if you can save half an hour a day for everyone in your department you deserve to be a company hero – not bad for an initiative well within your competence and costing little or no money!

PARKINSON, PARETO AND PRIORITIES

Parkinson's famous First Law states that 'work expands to fill the time available for its completion', which means that if you allow an hour for a job it will take you an hour to complete it.

Try shrinking the work by allowing yourself half an hour to do it. You will almost certainly come up with a better and faster way of completing the task and one thing you will *not* do will be to waste time by aiming for perfection – in every job.

The 'Law of diminishing returns' applies to the investment of time in a task. You might be able to improve a job by spending the extra half hour on it, but by how much – and is it worth it? It's a judgement call.

Of course, we are not saying that people like surgeons and aircraft mechanics should not take time to aim for perfection; of course they should. What we are saying is that they should not waste time trying to, say, draft a perfect letter, time that would be better spent on surgery or aircraft maintenance.

Us the *Pareto Principle* to help you decide. Economist Wilfredo Pareto discovered that in Italy 20 per cent of the population controlled 80 per cent of the country's material wealth. Later, other people noticed that the same proportions applied to many different situations and that, for example, 20 per cent of a newspaper contains 80 per cent of its news, 20 per cent of a company's clients account for 80 per cent of its sales, 20 per cent of a salesforce does 80 per cent of the work and so on.

Also known as the 20–80 Rule, the Pareto Principle indicates that 20 per cent of your effort will produce 80 per cent of the effect. For example, if you were dropping a note to a friend, grammar, vocabulary and layout which were 80 per cent perfect might be completely acceptable, but if you were writing out a job application you would consider the investment of more time and effort totally justifiable. In both cases, training and experience will enable you to get nearer to perfection for the same expenditure of time and effort.

Sound time management is very often the triumph of pragmatism over perfectionism.

- *Don't work harder.* Work better, and more effectively.
- *Don't worry.* Turn your worries into problems which can be solved by you, or with the help of other people. Worry is one of the world's greatest time-wasters.
- *Don't feel guilty* about not getting *everything* perfect. Ration your effort by getting only the really important things perfect. This could mean a battle against your conditioning. Schools used to make children aim for perfection when tracing maps of Norway showing every tiny fiord and inlet. As a result they had no time to learn anything about Norway except that it has a much-indented coastline.
- *Don't procrastinate.* The old saw 'Never put off till tomorrow what you can do today' makes sense, especially when taken in conjunction with the other one which asserts that 'tomorrow never comes'.

THE THIEF OF TIME

Procrastination is the tendency to put *everything* off until tomorrow. It's a sickness which begins with indecision and, if not halted, progresses from chaos to paralysis. Fortunately, in the early stages at least, it is curable.

If you never procrastinate you are a rare human being. Most of us find ourselves inventing reasons for not doing things immediately, hive off unpleasant jobs, leave things until the last minute and let bad situations lurch on without taking corrective action until it's too late.

The trouble with procrastination is that it is contagious, which means that a procrastinating front-line manager will infect a whole department. Start putting everything off and pretty soon the whole of your staff will be day dreaming, welcoming interruptions, taking extra long coffee and meal breaks and using perfectionism – 'We're still waiting for the Outer Mongolian figures' – as just one element in a battery of excuses for not getting started.

FEAR OF FAILURE

One of the main reasons for procrastination is the often unacknowledged fear that we may fail. By not acting, we are protecting ourselves against failure.

There's even a superstitious fear that by acting we may provoke the thing we fear. That's why people sometimes refrain from 'phoning their bosses to ask for a decision, even though they know that the enquiry will not affect the outcome one way or the other.

Having failed in the past is another cause of procrastination. It takes courage to face the fear that we may fail again and to tell ourselves that this is a new game and a chance to show that we have learned from our experience.

MANAGERS' BLOCK

Authors are particularly prone to procrastination, which they prefer to call writers' block. In their case, procrastination comes down to looking at reams of blank paper, cursing their lack of inspiration and hoping that someone will call to drag them out for a drink or sell them a vacuum cleaner.

Journalists, on the other hand, who sometimes suffer from the same complaint, have found the answer – *just start*. Once you have something down on paper you can improve it. If you have written nothing, all you have is blank paper.

The reason why many authors are badly affected by writers' block is that, in most cases, the delivery date set for their manuscript is months ahead. By contrast, most journalists can deal with writers' block because on a big story they not only have a deadline to meet but they may have the editor standing at their elbow, impatient for copy. Instead of staring at blank paper or a blank screen, they just start.

Sufferers from managers' block need only to consider the difference.

THE DIFFERENCE IS THE DEADLINE

A goal without a deadline isn't really a goal at all – it's an invitation to procrastinate.

If you have not been set a deadline, set one for yourself. Make it a reasonable one and divide it into stages with a separate deadline for each.

Use the PACA PACA sequence. Plan the action you intend to take and then *act*. This means that you have started the management motor, energy is flowing and you can move on to the *control* stage to modify and improve, before acting again.

It sounds obvious, but if you don't *act* you have nothing to modify and improve.

Remember that a plan is only a plan, so there is usually no reason to treat it as sacrosanct, or to wait until you know your action is going to be perfect before starting. Once again, because it is so important, the answer to the problem of getting started is *just start*.

DON'T WAIT TO DELEGATE

Delegation is a perfect example of a managerial action which can be totally inhibited by procrastination.

Most of us can think of a hundred excuses to put off the single course of action that can save us more time than any other.

It's also a good example of 'offensive' time management, but 'defensive' time management can be just as effective. You should, for instance, be on your guard against members of your staff who try to delegate things to *you*, often manipulating you so subtly – 'I'd like your opinion on this' or 'This job really needs someone with your experience and qualifications' – that you finish up doing half their work.

Known officially as 'retrograde delegation', this ploy used to be known, in the North of England at least, as 'playing Johnny's mother', and was the classic way of getting out of everything from washing up – 'I'll only break things' – to writing reports – 'I'm afraid I'd make a mess of it'.

Your defence is to encourage people to do things on their own and coach them where necessary. Ask them to write a memo explaining their problem and why they don't think they can do the job. This could sort out the people who are trying it on and identify any real problems. If people do have genuine problems, suggest, encourage, teach but *don't* do the job for them. One day they will have to stop being spoon-fed and make decisions on their own. Why not today?

INTERRUPTIONS – AND HOW TO INTERRUPT THEM

Another good example of defensive time management is the ability to protect your own time against interruptions.

Many managers spend more than a third of their working lives dealing with interruptions or recovering their concentration after it has been broken or disrupted. This could mean that you are spending weeks or even months in every year battling against what are in effect attacks on your time.

Of course, some of the interruptions are warranted, but there are ways of making sure that you get to know in time if the building is on fire or if somebody needs your signature on a million pound contract. Most other interruptions are either unnecessary or can wait till a non-disruptive time – like a regular meeting.

Try listing *all* interruptions to your work in an average day as 'useless', 'non-urgent' or 'vital', noting in each case the person concerned, the reason, and the time taken up.

The list will tell you who and what caused most interruptions – including the ones you caused yourself by deciding, for instance, to 'phone your home – and will almost certainly indicate that only around 20 per cent of all interruptions are justified.

This does not mean that you must never 'phone your home or get up to have a stretch or take time off to greet an old friend who's in town for an hour, any more than it means you should give up coffee breaks, but it does indicate that there is great scope for improvement. It also points out where your defences are weakest.

DEFENCE IN DEPTH

Plan your defence. Enlist your secretary and train her in anti-interruption techniques, including:

- not letting anyone into your office without an appointment, including your friends from other departments. Don't have her lie needlessly. You don't have to be 'in a meeting' to be busy. Do get her to ask people what they want and suggest 'phoning them when you are free;
- keeping even vital interruptions to a minimum. Practise interrupting interruptions with 'important' 'phone calls;
- being tactful. Students who 'sport their oak' don't offend people because, by closing their outer door, they have effectively given notice that they are working;
- defending you against superiors who interrupt. This can be tough but get your secretary to tell them you are working on a time management system which could save the company thousands of pounds and that you will be preparing a report in due course. Meanwhile, could she take a message or make an appointment?

Don't loiter in 'no man's land' when walking from your office to another. You are asking for that 'Could I just have a word?' which turns out to last 20 minutes. Incidentally, one good reason for walking to someone else's office is the *control* factor. You can leave when *you* want to.

LEARN TO SAY NO

You don't have to snarl but you do have to learn to say *no*, not only to interruptions but to most appeals from people who want you to do their work for them, to most invitations to nip out for a drink and to nearly everyone who has 'just dropped in for a chat'.

Identify people on your staff or otherwise who want to use *you* as yet another excuse not to get started, as in 'I got stuck talking to Mike and before I knew it the afternoon had gone'. Tell them to go off and join Procrastinators Anonymous – 'My name is T. M. Pussfugit and I am a procrastinator . . .' That way you can get them to leave you – laughing.

THE CONTROL QUOTIENT

Very high. As indicated, most of the time management initiatives we have looked at so far have a high *control* factor. Many needless interruptions are caused by your own staff and can be easily screened out. Others, like interruptions by superiors, can be influenced.

HOW WILL YOU KNOW YOU HAVE SUCCEEDED?

You will know that you have made a good start on time management when you have time to think and plan your own work and that of your department. You should also be feeling less harassed and more in charge of your own destiny.

Changing your attitude to time will have begun to pay more tangible dividends in the form of higher productivity and you will be looking for more ways to manage this precious resource, not just for yourself but for everyone on your staff.

SUMMARY

- How you could be 'cheating' your company by wasting or misusing time they are paying for at manager's rates.
- The frightening costs of not managing time efficiently.

- Time management as a cost-effective front-line initiative yielding immediate and visible results, which can be put in place by any manager.
- How much is your company really paying for your time? How much does a wasted 'phone call really cost? How much time can you save?
- Parkinson, Pareto and priorities or how to get more done in half the time.
- The thief of time and how to arrest it.
- Interruptions and how to interrupt them.
- How you can save time by learning to say *no*.

TWELVE

Time and the Hot Department

Managing your own time can increase your productivity and efficiency, but managing your people's time and coaching them in efficient time management can work miracles.

Mind you, unless you make it absolutely clear to your staff that time management will benefit everyone, it could seem like a crafty management ploy to get people to work harder.

Remember that other people are not you and will not be motivated in exactly the same way. However, most people will appreciate being less stressed, having time to spare, even when deadlines are tight, and only very rarely having to take work home.

Remember too that other people's time is valuable to them, as well as to the company. If you ever want to use more of it than you have paid for, you can beg for it, buy it or borrow it, but you mustn't steal it. Asking a favour every now and again is fine, as is paid overtime or 'time off in lieu', but making people work after quitting time when even a minute can cause them to miss their transport home is demotivating.

Managing time correctly should mean that you rarely need to ask people to put in more than the normal working day and that in itself could be a considerable saving in expenditure.

GREEN TIME AND RED TIME

One way of saving time for the whole of your staff is by planning interruptions in order to limit them and the disruption they can cause.

IML, for example, have instituted a system of 'Green Time' and 'Red Time' and have let everyone who is in regular communication with them know which times they would like them to consider red – meaning 'no interruptions please' – and which green.

Allot times to suit your department's need. At IML, Red Time is from 9.00 till 9.45 a.m., which enables everyone to settle down, to open all correspondence, to decide on the priorities of anything requiring action and to plan their day.

In addition to the informal request to outsiders, there is a ban on internal 'phone calls in Red Time, after which everyone moves into Green Time, when interruptions are part of the normal working day and are dealt with by filtering and by limiting the time they take. There are also half-hour periods of Red Time in the middle and at the end of each day.

Another way in which you and your staff can limit interruptions is to install a simple 'traffic light' system on your office door, plus those of your senior people and of conference rooms, to indicate that intending interrupters will either do so 'at their peril' or risk nothing worse than a frown.

Use your own 'traffic lights' to match your personal efficiency curve.

RESPECTING THE BIOLOGICAL CLOCK

You will have noticed that, as a rule, there are some times when you work better than at others and you could ask your secretary to modify your Red and Green times to match your 'biological clock'.

This varies from person to person. Most people achieve maximum efficiency at around 10 a.m., with another surge around 5 p.m., so it is safe to make general arrangements with this in mind. However, if you are one of those individuals who peak at different times, take this into account when planning your day. If, for example, you fade for half an hour or so after lunch, this would not be the best time to schedule important meetings.

Take regular short breaks. Psychiatrists who spend a '45-

minute hour' with patients and use the rest of the time for relaxation, or less demanding work like 'phone calls or letter writing, know what they are doing.

One German film producer we knew, who rarely spent more than a couple of hours in bed and invariably got through a phenomenal amount of work, told us that his secret was a five-minute zizz that topped up his energy level for the next hour or so.

You could find it easier to walk around for five minutes in every sixty, have a quick chat or tackle an easy job. Topping up your concentration is *not* a waste of time if it turns poor time into prime production time.

Make sure your staff take short breaks too. Watch yourself and others for signs of overwork like tiredness, frustration, inefficiency and bad temper. If you, or they, are overworking you are not managing your time correctly. Stress can kill. A complete break, a couple of days 'light duty', followed by a change in the way you handle time, could prevent you from losing *all* the time you have left.

DELEGATION

Delegation to individuals and groups will save your time and enable you to work more effectively, but don't forget that there are almost certainly some people on your staff whose time is more valuable than that of their fellow-employees.

To save your top people's time, delegate tasks to the lowest person on the ladder who is capable of doing them. This will stretch the person concerned and free those above them for more important work.

TIME AND THE ORGANIZED DESK

Do you have a messy desk and an office that looks like the aftermath of a hurricane? You could be wasting a lot of time searching for lost files, missing reports and elusive pens.

Tidy up, file rubbish like junk mail in the WPB. Use a separate box as 'limbo' for documents you 'might just need' and clear it at regular intervals.

Arrange your desk space so that the things you need most frequently are readily to hand. If you are right handed, your phone should be on your left with notepaper, pens and so on to your right. Try to keep the space in front of you free.

Within arm's reach you should have a three-drawer filing cabinet for documents that are (a) *urgent*, (b) *important* and (c) to be filed or forwarded to somebody else.

'Close' open plan offices if need be with dividers, book cases or pot plants to mark out your own work station and to make sure anyone who wants to reach it has to get past your secretary first.

If you have a closed office, try to arrange a 'creativity corner', even if it means bringing in an armchair from your home.

Involve your staff in desk and office organization. Check things like furniture, lighting, colours, and noise levels. You could save time and increase productivity by as much as 15 per cent.

TIME AND THE ORGANIZED WORKPLACE

If your offices or shop floor look like a disturbed ant hill, a careful look at the ways in which people, papers and materials move around the workplace could save your department a lot of time.

This is an excellent front-line management initiative which involves little expenditure and has a high *control* factor. It's also a good illustration of the fact that in most cases *planning is cheaper than acting*. In this case, for instance, it costs a lot less in terms of disruption to *plan* ways of moving people and things around the workplace than it does to start shifting furniture and changing work patterns until you get things right.

Plan Use a workflow diagram and begin by establishing what is happening at the moment. To do this, all you need is a rough diagram of your floor space showing all the fixed objects like doors and pillars. It might save time to have a few of these diagrams run off.

Make cardboard cut-outs of movable objects like desks, filing cabinets, machines and so on; put them in their current positions and make a 'Before' diagram by drawing in the movements of people and things. If the lines begin at one door, touch each desk in turn and in order, flowing purposefully around the workplace like the rails of a model railway layout you have no problem. If, on the other hand, your diagram looks like a child's scribble with hairpins, crossed lines, reversals and circles, an inefficient workflow could be wasting a lot of time.

With the process in mind, try shifting the cut-outs around to reduce unnecessary movements and then draw another flow diagram. You may find that there has been some improvement but that there are still a great many untidy lines rather than an orderly progression. On the ground, this could mean that Peter is regularly walking round half a dozen desks – or perhaps even into another building – to hand over documents to Jane, who then has to carry them back again for Peter's approval.

Could you shift Peter's or Jane's workstations closer together?

Are there any stages in the process itself which are redundant? Check especially for things which 'have always been done' in a particular way.

Now could be a good time to 'involve to solve', by setting up an *ad hoc* team of some or all of the people concerned to see if they can improve the flow of their work still further. People who are involved in finding solutions in this way will be keen to make them work.

Act Move the furniture. Try out the new system for a couple of days.

Control Has time been saved? Is there room for further improvement? How could the plan be amended? Find the *critical path* – the shortest way, in terms of time, to complete the process.

Act Make the necessary changes and adjustments. Redraw the flow diagram.

TIME AND THE ORGANIZED WORKFORCE

Save time by using lists yourself and by coaching your people to use them. They are the backbone of any sound organization, have a high *control* factor and cost virtually nothing.

Different coloured pens are a simple way of coding things like tasks in terms of priority and you could make the code department-wide.

Use a loose-leaf, rolling diary system to list the things you have to do each day and cross them off as you deal with them. Establish a forward planning system with a call forward mechanism for as far ahead as you wish to plan.

Use the diary to record deadlines for yourself and others. That way you won't need to remind yourself that a specific day – and even a specific time – are more motivating than 'towards the end of next month'. Set intermediate targets, using the diary to keep a check on progress.

Use rewards – a drink after work or even a simple thank you – for deadlines met. Mark each entry with its appropriate file code number and change the colour coding of this if an intermediate deadline has not been met.

Make as many separate lists as you need of people, tasks or materials. Your memory could be infallible but can you say the same for every member of your staff?

FLOWCHARTING – A VISUAL RECORD

Flowcharting is a visual record of a task which shows:

- *inputs* – the people, machines and materials used;
- *changes* – the ways in which the inputs are transformed;
- *output* – the results of the transformation.

It enables you and your staff to see at a glance what stage a particular job has reached and by indicating where effort is needed can often save a lot of time.

As you may want your staff and perhaps people from other departments to use your flowcharts, it makes sense to use the standard symbols from the beginning.

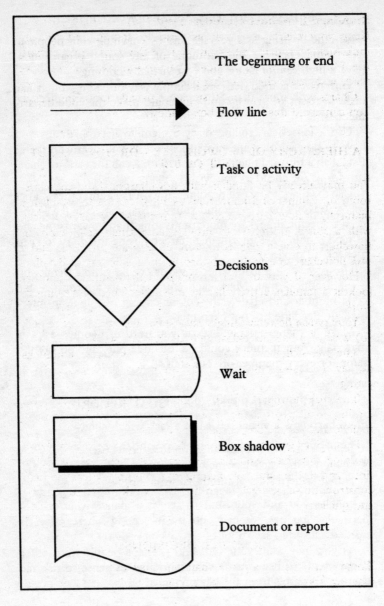

The beginning or end

Flow line

Task or activity

Decisions

Wait

Box shadow

Document or report

Standard flowchart symbols (*See p. 130*)

Keep your charts as simple as possible. If you find you are introducing too many details into one of the steps on your chart, use a 'box shadow' on the main chart to indicate that you have made a separate chart for that particular step.

Charts with more than 20 steps are usually too complicated. You can avoid this by using box shadows.

A HIERARCHY OF FLOWCHARTS – OR HOW TO GET OUT OF BED

You may already be familiar with flowcharting from the classroom or seminar and know how useful it can be to establish a hierarchy of flowcharts ranging from the strategic to the tactical, with a *system* flowchart to provide an overall view, a *process* flowchart to give a detailed picture of separate processes and a *task* flowchart to examine any process in the system in detail.

However, if you are not too happy with them, take another look at a familiar activity like getting out of bed and going to work.

Your *system* flowchart might have steps like (a) get out of bed, (b) wash, (c) have breakfast and (d) travel to work.

The *process* flowchart takes one step like 'breakfast' and looks at, say, (a) setting the table, (b) preparing breakfast and (c) eating.

The *task* flowchart could examine preparing breakfast: (a) cutting bread, (b) making toast, (c) putting on butter and marmalade and (d) making coffee.

Persuading your family, if you have one, to help establish a morning flowchart would almost certainly help to save some time, and in the same way getting your workplace team to help construct flowcharts will mean that they work more efficiently – and quicker.

DECISIONS! DECISIONS!

There's an old story about a chap who goes to the doctor complaining about his stressful job and who turns out to be not a captain of industry but a pea-sorter. 'Decisions, decisions, all day decisions,' he whimpers, 'it's driving me insane.'

Of course managers have to take more important decisions than those involved in sizing peas every working day. In fact, it is a major part of their job and many of them find it stressful and time-consuming.

To save time in decision-making, tackle each decision methodically.

- *Use the 'W' questions* to decide *who* requires you to make a decision and who stands to lose or to benefit and by how much. *What* it is that you have to decide? *Why* is a decision needed? *Where* and, more importantly, *when* is a decision needed?
- *Grade decisions* as (a) very important, (b) important and (c) unimportant. This is an essential factor in time management as many people devote as much, or even more, time and energy to unimportant decisions as they do to major ones.
- *List* all available options.
- *Make a mental decision* based on intuition. List the pros and cons, and use the cons list to argue the case against your intuitive decision. This will often give you a new view of the problem.
- *Set a deadline* for decision-making based on the importance of the decision. 'Thinking things over' is not dithering, provided you have a decision deadline.
- *Act.* 'Decide to decide', quickly if the decision is an emergency one, and then implement the decision. In most cases an incorrect decision, which can be amended if necessary, is better than no decision at all.

DIVIDE AND CONQUER

If your decision is to undertake a project, divide it up into sub-projects to make the job more manageable. Allot a portion of time to each step – if appropriate one day to each – to give you a grip on time expenditure.

Dividing jobs in this way enables you to spot possible problem areas and to take steps to tackle them in advance. It will also help you to call a halt to non-viable projects before you start, rather than half-way through them, which could mean enormous savings in time – and money.

SPEED READING – HOW TO CUT READING TIME BY 100 PER CENT

As a front-line manager it is almost certain that you now have to read more in the workplace than you did as a member of the rank and file. In fact, you could be drowning in an ocean of memos, letters, reports, files, trade magazines, specialist books and the rest, apart from your need to be better informed about national and international news, economic trends and so on.

Obviously, it will help if you are able to read faster but there are a couple of things you can do before speeeding up your reading – like deciding what you *need* to read and not reading the rest at all.

YOUR FRIEND THE WASTE PAPER BASKET

A good half of the processed Amazon rainforest that drops on your desk every day can be sent for recycling without your having to read it. Instead you can:

- get your secretary to divide all correspondence into such categories as 'obvious rubbish', 'secretary can handle', 'should look at', 'important' and 'urgent'. *Delegate* the first two piles to her as soon as you are certain that her selection is accurate;
- skim the 'should look at' pile. Be ruthless. If you don't *need* to read it – don't read it! Put it in the waste paper basket. If there is a heading that could be interesting, use a highlighter pen to mark it for attention when you have a moment to spare;
- use colour code highlighting to mark out vital sections of the

'important' and 'urgent' correspondence – another job to *delegate* to your secretary after coaching.

Instead of facing a daunting pile of correspondence you could finish up with a few paragraphs to read.

Don't overload your secretary but, if your time management coaching leaves her with time to spare, she could find it interesting to go through the trade magazines and newspapers you would otherwise not get round to reading, highlighting items of interest.

TABOO OR NOT TABOO?

Marking books used to be almost a hanging offence but you should now get rid of this conditioning as far as your own books are concerned, especially those relating to your work.

Use different coloured highlighters to mark passages of text that interest you, rather than spend time making notes. That way you can remind yourself of all the important points in a colour grouping in a matter of minutes.

This book, for instance, is designed to be read fast and, where possible, is arranged in bite-sized chunks so that all you need do as you read it is to tick or highlight the cross-heading you want to return to.

If you want to speed up things still further you will have to learn speed reading.

SPEED READING

Most children still learn to read by pronouncing each letter d-o-g = dog until they can recognize the whole word. They progress to the stage where they are able to read sentences aloud, then to the stage where their lips move as they read and from there to the stage where they hear the words in their head.

Some people do not move on from here, although anyone who reads a great deal will have speeded up a little, perhaps without realizing it. You may have noticed for instance that often, when turning a page, you can guess the first word on the next page before reading it. This is because you have become accustomed to reading frequently occurring phrases and especially pairs of words in blocks. If 'eggs and . . .' are the last words on a page you would expect the first word on the next page to be 'bacon'.

Speed reading takes things a stage further by teaching you to read in blocks.

If you are not able to take a course in speed reading for the moment you can speed up tremendously by splitting pages of text into three columns with two vertical lines and practising reading by moving your eyes only three times per line. When you can do this easily, divide pages with a single line and read with only two eye movements per line. After a while you will not need the lines and you could be reading more than twice as fast without any loss of concentration.

BRAINSTORM FOR SPEED

'Involve to solve' by coaching your staff in time management and by getting *them* to suggest how time can be saved. They could come up with something as simple and effective as the Mars company's understandably short *stand-up* morning meetings. Use brainstorming to elicit ideas on how people can save time on their own tasks. Introduce an element of competition where appropriate. Reward time-savers, perhaps with time itself. If they have saved a couple of hours per day, for example, an early finish at the weekend might be a suitable recompense.

THE CONTROL QUOTIENT

Time management is an ideal front-line initiative because of its high *control* quotient and its overall application. Properly handled it is enough in itself to make yours a 'hot department'.

HOW WILL YOU KNOW YOU HAVE SUCCEEDED?

You will know you have succeeded in managing your time efficiently *when people are prepared to offer you more for it.*

SUMMARY

- Why you should become a time management coach.
- Green Time and Red Time, the 'lights' that help you control information traffic and cut down interruptions.
- How to save time by relaxing and by respecting your 'biological clock'.
- How to save time by organizing your desk, your office, your workplace and your staff.
- Flowcharting – how to identify possible time savings by making a visual record of tasks and sub-tasks.
- How to save reading time by *not* reading.
- Speed reading – how to make a start by doubling your reading speed and that of everyone in your department.

PART FOUR

Communications

THIRTEEN

Communications and the Front-Line Manager

Front-line managers have always needed to communicate but, once industry got past the 'Haul that rope and lift that bale' stage and instructions became more technical, those managers in direct contact with the rank and file were forced to improve their communication skills.

Today, as processes become even more complex and employees increasingly sophisticated and involved, the ability to communicate effectively has become not merely desirable but essential.

In this information age, it is no longer enough for front-line managers to be able to act as conduits between senior management and the workforce. They need the skills which will enable them to communicate both vertically, between the management and the front line, and horizontally with their fellow-managers.

Communication skills make it possible for them not only to pass on instructions and report back to senior management, but to carry out a wide range of managerial activities including motivation, delegation and presentation, as well as putting into place their own initiatives and those of senior management.

THE TRAGEDY OF ERRORS

By contrast, managers who fail to communicate well leave themselves open to any number of annoying and costly errors, misunderstandings and lost opportunities. The smallest error in communication can have consequences totally out of proportion with the original mistake. Cumulative errors in communication have caused wars, lost major battles and resulted in industrial calamities on the scale of the Three Mile Island disaster. They can play havoc with the work of your department.

This is why it is imperative that you are able to communicate effectively with individuals ranging from chief executive officers to cleaners, and with groups ranging from senior management to your own departmental teams.

Unfortunately, global communication of this sort is complicated by the fact that every individual has his or her own language.

LANGUAGE – A MAJOR COMMUNICATION PROBLEM

There's an old saying to the effect that Britain and America are 'two nations divided by a common language' but, while many words and expressions have different meanings in the two countries, this is a minor problem when compared to the fact that very few words mean exactly the same thing for two individual English-speakers, whatever their nationality.

Fortunately, there are enough words with approximately the same meaning to make communication possible, but this can lead to a sense of false security unless we realize that the way people react to our attempts to communicate with them will be governed by their background – especially their early childhood – their culture, their education and their experience.

Even body language, which seems as though it should be international and intercultural, can be a potential minefield of misunderstandings. There are communities, for example, where a nod of the head means no instead of yes, while in others indicating by gestures that you want two of something can have disastrous consequences.

As a front-line manager, whatever form of communication you are using, it is essential to bear in mind the manager's joke syndrome and to be aware that when you communicate with your staff, everything you say or write 'counts double'. This means, for example, that while praise from you will be doubly gratifying, an ill-chosen word can be doubly hurtful and demotivating.

THE PERILS OF THE 'GREAT COMMUNICATORS'

Even being an officially acknowledged 'good communicator' is no guarantee that you will be able to 'get through' to others, and many people with impressive degrees find communication difficult, either because they try to be too clever or because they remain resolutely on the wrong wavelength. We remember, for instance, brilliant and articulate barristers with a wonderful command of English who were unable to communicate with their clients because they spoke a completely different language.

As a manager you should be aware of any possible language gap and be especially careful not to use technical language and jargon not shared by the people you are talking to.

Of course, new managers should be aware of the technical language appropriate to their speciality and have a wide general vocabulary, but they should refrain from flaunting this knowledge unless they are certain they will be understood.

Communication can be complicated but fortunately front-line managers are ideally situated to become 'communications chameleons', able to switch wavelengths at will.

At the same time there are a few basic rules which make it possible to avoid many communication errors.

THE CARDINAL RULE

Communication of every type is fraught with hazards but, whatever sort of communication you engage in – and whether you are speaking or writing to individuals or to groups – there is one rule which will help you to cut through the confusion and to convey your meaning clearly.

KEEP IT SIMPLE!

The historian and novelist Barbara Tuchman once asserted that unless she wrote in such a way that everyone was able to understand her she had failed. If people don't understand *you*, you have failed. To help you keep it simple, use the 'W' questions.

ASK THE 'W' QUESTIONS

Before communicating at all, ask yourself:

- *who* do you want to communicate with? This will guide you in your choice of vocabulary and expression. Ask yourself, for example, what national newspaper the individuals and groups might read. Newspapers which cannot communicate with their readership cannot survive. They have to be good at it;
- *what* do you want to communicate? Be clear what you want to say or write and plan every communication before you start;
- *why* do you want to communicate? Asking this question can save time and effort by helping you to eliminate unnecessary communications, especially those of the 'we've always submitted a daily report to Mr Farquaharson' type';
- *where* should the communication take place? An important question for verbal communications. Calling people into your office, rather than criticising them in front of their colleagues, is a case in point;
- *when* should the communication be made? Whether you want to communicate with your staff or your CEO, five minutes to five on a Friday evening is probably not the best time to choose.

The answers to these questions may also influence your choice of *how* you communicate and, for example, whether you write, fax or pick up the 'phone.

A SIMPLE WAY TO BECOME A BETTER COMMUNICATOR

Most communication skills take time to acquire but there is one way in which you can improve communications immediately and that is by changing your attitude, where necessary, toward the people you speak or write to.

Good manners are the key to good communications and, in the first instance, many people find it helpful to 'promote' the individuals or groups with whom they are communicating. This mental promotion not only 'strokes' the people concerned but dictates a more respectful approach and a more careful choice of vocabulary than might otherwise have been the case.

Examine your attitudes and those of your staff for possible prejudices and change your language accordingly. If you, or they, frequently use words like 'all' or 'everybody' as in 'All senior managers are autocratic swine' or 'Everybody in the packing department is lazy' your attitudes are a barrier to effective communication.

ARE YOU OK?

Psychologists identify four basic attitudes:

- *I'm OK – you're not OK* people have often been treated badly as children. This attitude emerges in communication situations as a tendency to blame other people, to humiliate them or to give them bad service or poor work;
- *I'm not OK – you're OK* people often feel powerless and have low self-esteem. They are frequently depressive and their communications are hampered by shyness or exaggerated humility;
- *I'm not OK – you're not OK* people are often depressed to the point of desperation. Their communications are usually confused and lacking in direction;
- *I'm OK – you're OK* people are 'winners', conscious of their own worth and that of other people. Their ego state is resolutely *adult* and, because they seek to win without causing other people to lose, their communications are direct, constructive and helpful.

DETECTING ATTITUDES

One way of detecting people's attitudes in order to improve communications with individuals and groups is to learn how to interpret body language.

Some body language is deliberate and few people, for instance, would misinterpret the significance of a raised clenched fist or a cupped hand behind the ear.

Most body language, however, is unconscious and it is this which makes it interesting for the manager who needs to be able to interpret other people's moods and attitudes before making decisions.

Body signals can be ambiguous – folded arms for instance could mean that you are unreceptive or merely that you are resting. The answer is to make sure that at least three signals are communicating the same thing. For example, if someone is sitting at their desk with their arms folded in front of them, shoulders raised and head lowered, the chances are that you are looking at someone who is really unhappy.

THE EYES HAVE IT

Eyes send out strong signals; dilated pupils, for example, can indicate interest, frankness, honesty or relaxation, while contracted pupils – provided they are not indicating that the light is too strong – can signal lack of interest, hostility, or distrust.

Mouths and eyebrows are also important, but perhaps the clearest signals come from people's posture. A person who leans backward when standing is usually defensive or mistrustful, while a person who leans forward is anxious to dominate or be insistent.

People who stand straight, by contrast, are in control, straightforward and 'happy in their skin'.

Watch too for people whose bodies are bent slightly forward, indicating friendship and concern, or those people who are literally 'puffed-up' with pride and self-importance.

THE TV TUTOR

If you wish to progress beyond the ABC of body language you almost certainly have an excellent tutor in your living room.

Watch the television news for examples of hostile body language of individuals and groups, and look at drama to see how actors use body language consciously and unconsciously to express or conceal their feelings. If you have a video recorder it could help if you watch things once or twice, both with and without the sound.

As you watch, bear in mind that you too send out body language signals which other people are able to receive, either consciously or unconsciously. Practise using body language to indicate, say, imperturbability or acute interest.

TELEPHONING AS A FINE ART

Most managers spend several hours a day talking to people on the 'phone but not all of them are able to do so effectively.

Of course, anyone can dial and speak into a 'phone, but unless you are able to project yourself and your wishes over the wire you are wasting half of the 'phone's capabilities.

Tele-sales people, for instance, some of whom are very good indeed, spend a long time acquiring their skills but there are things you can do to improve 'phone communications quickly.

Thinking of the 'phone as an instrument will help you to use it well and to get the most from it.

Signalling by means of body language, for example, to someone who can't see you sounds ridiculous, but in fact the best way to use a 'phone effectively is to act into it.

Try smiling, gesturing with your arms and hands, raising your eyebrows and so on, when you are on the 'phone. Like other electronic devices, 'phones seem capable of picking up gestures of this sort, much as they exaggerate people's accents.

Use a tape recorder attached to another telephone to hear what you really sound like on the 'phone. Practise projecting honesty, excitement, doubt and so on until you can put over nuances like cautious optimism or vague doubt, merely by changing your tone. Once again, listening to actors on TV can help.

HOW TO IMPROVE YOUR WHOLE DEPARTMENT – OVERNIGHT

Try getting the whole of your staff to take part in an experiment in 'Phoning as a Fine Art'.

Explain that the 'phone, although a super-sensitive instrument, can be fooled in so far as people at the other end of the line cannot see that the person they are speaking to is feeling dreadful, has had a spat with a colleague or lost an important file.

This makes every 'phone call a chance to project a vibrant, alert, helpful image and to put themselves over as 'winners' – 'can-do' people who, while fully prepared to help others, are confident that people will be only too glad to help them.

Begin by getting them to put a child's version of a smiling face – a circle with dots for eyes and an upturned curve for the mouth – by their 'phone.

Find out how they normally answer the 'phone and, if necessary, coach them to use an upbeat tone and a standard reply that offers information and assistance rather than merely saying 'Hello'. For instance, 'Hello, this is Jane Roberts' is an improvement; 'Hello. Jane Roberts, Accounts Department, here' is better; and 'Hello. Accounts Department. Jane Roberts here. How can I help you?' is better still.

You could even delegate the job of 'phone coach and offer a small prize for the 'Phone Personality' of the week.

THE CONTROL QUOTIENT

Communications is an area with a high *control* quotient for new managers and one that offers big dividends for the effort expended. You can improve your own communication skills and ensure better internal and external communications in your department by coaching and ensuring that standards, once attained, are kept up.

HOW WILL YOU KNOW YOU HAVE SUCCEEDED?

Improved communication will change the face of your department and make it more efficient. It will also change for the better the way in which your department is perceived by your internal and external customers.

Coaching your people to adopt a pleasant and positive telephone manner will give them more confidence and increase their ability to get things done. At the same time, their 'up beat' attitude on the phone will spread to the rest of their working day and they will begin to feel like 'can-do' people.

As front-line manager you will know you have succeeded when you begin to feel that you are in charge of a smooth-running efficient machine.

SUMMARY

- Why today's more complex processes and more sophisticated employees make communication an essential skill for front-line managers.
- The perils of poor communication including the possibility of costly errors and missed opportunities.
- How to cope with communication 'language' problems by becoming a 'communications chameleon'.
- The manager's joke syndrome again and why your communications as manager have double the effect they may once have had.
- Why some 'great communicators' fail. When not to use jargon and why you should avoid the temptation to employ the specialist language of your particular élite when talking to people who might not understand.
- How to detect other people's attitudes by interpreting their body language. How to project the feelings you wish to convey by using body language yourself.
- 'Phoning as a fine art. A skill that can improve the work of your whole department.

FOURTEEN

Talking to Individuals

Front-line managers who are in daily contact with their staff and their internal and external customers spend up to half their working lives talking to people.

Unfortunately, according to some experts, many of them waste almost two hours a day of this time, which means they could be losing more than two months a year because of poor verbal communication skills.

This is largely because most schools concentrate on reading and writing and devote little or no time to teaching their pupils how to talk while, significantly, many of those who acquire verbal communication skills do so in their own time as members of dramatic or debating societies.

The feeling seems to be that 'anyone can talk', so there is no need to teach them how to do so. This is rather like saying that, since most people will swim if thrown in at the deep end of a pool, there is no need for swimming tuition.

CUT THE CACKLE

The first moves towards effective verbal communication in the workplace should be directed towards cutting down, where feasible, the time you spend talking to people, by planning and by making yourself more effective.

- *Ask* the 'W' questions and prepare for workplace conversations – as opposed to chats – by deciding *who* it is you are going to talk to and exactly what you are going to say. Make sure you have all the information, including any documents you may need, to hand. Write down all the topics

you intend to raise so that you can tick them off as they
are dealt with.

- *Ask* people you know are going to present you with a lot of
  facts and figures to drop you a note listing them before you
  meet. This saves you having to take notes during the
  conversation or rely on your memory. Of course, it is
  possible to tape-record important conversations but you
  won't want to play the whole tape merely to find a couple
  of elusive facts.
- *Don't* waste words on chit-chat. Comedians can make a living
  by piling up superfluous details and ridiculous digressions
  but, when the workplace meter is running for both parties,
  conversations are costly and it pays to get to the point.
- *Do* take time to explain things properly. Be patient. Other
  people are not you and do not share your background,
  experience or knowledge. Too many conversations are
  'repeats' due to not getting things right the first time. Make
  absolutely certain, especially when giving instructions, that
  the other person has understood you completely. A couple
  of questions before they leave your office will save people
  coming back to you for clarification and could prevent
  costly errors.

THE LOST ART OF LISTENING

Zeno – who sounds more like one of the Marx Brothers than a
Greek philosopher – asserted that 'The reason we have two ears
and only one mouth is that we need to listen more and talk less'.

In fact, managers can apply the 80–20 rule most of the time,
by letting the other person do up to 80 oer cent of the talking
while they listen – actively.

Active listening means:

- *paying attention*, not merely to every word another person
  says but also to their body language, and deciphering any
  concealed messages. It means resisting the temptation to
  switch over to 'automatic'. This is the mode in which you
  instruct your mind to scan for 'trigger' words and to 'record'

what the other person is saying, while you think of other things.

It is a facility which comes in handy in some domestic situations and many political meetings but it should not be used in the workplace where the manager who is listening actively can make certain that the other person transmits all the relevant information, while holding them to the point and keeping time-wasting to the minimum.

When practised correctly this word rationing doesn't give the impression that you are in too much of a hurry to listen but, on the contrary, allows people to go away thinking – correctly – that you have taken plenty of time to consider carefully everything they had to say.

- *providing verbal and non-verbal feedback.* This is such an important element of conversation that TV interviewers often record 'noddies' of themselves nodding their heads sapiently or pursing their lips in thoughtful agreement – after the interviewee has left.
- *willingness to listen* to other points of view without 'jumping in'.

PACING

Once you have eliminated the unnecessary elements in your verbal communications and acquired the habit of active listening, including observing the person you are talking to, you should concentrate on 'pacing' the other person.

This means getting as close as possible to their 'wavelength' in order to achieve rapport and involves moving in the direction of the other person's body language, speech and feelings.

Some pacing occurs automatically between friends – especially lovers – who unconsciously mirror each other's posture, talk at the same speed and at the same pitch and enjoy discovering common attitudes.

Conscious pacing means adopting roughly the same stance as the other person, using a vocabulary close to theirs, while modifying your accent, if need be, to minimize contrast, and seeking areas of agreement.

WHEN NOT TO PACE

Don't try to pace angry or depressed people by matching their mood as this will only make things worse.

On the other hand, complete 'dis-pacing' can be equally wrong. A soft answer may 'turn away wrath' but if delivered in cool, measured tones it can make people madder than they were to begin with, while telling depressed people to 'buck up' in a cheery voice can make them feel suicidal.

Instead, show concern but switch their attention to a possible solution: 'I can see how that could be worrying you, Fred, and I understand how you feel. Why don't we put our heads together and see what we can do about it?'

Another difficult pacing situation can arise if you are working for a boss whose social, religious or political views are diametrically opposed to your own. The temptation to 'pace' the boss by echoing their views is strong, but in most cases it is better to keep quiet when they are sounding off and to pace on uncontroversial topics.

USE RUSE TO DE-FUSE

One way to 'de-fuse' angry people is to persuade them to pause for a few seconds. This only works if you can do it genuinely with something like, 'Hello, Freda, take a seat. I've been meaning to ask you to drop by so I could congratulate you on the way you handled the Robinson business. Now, what was it you wanted to see me about?'

In some cases, 'I was just going to have a drink; would you care for one?' can lower the temperature and enable you to begin pacing.

PACING AND DIS-PACING

Use pacing in most situations, not merely to de-fuse but to match people's enthusiasm and to mirror their excitement, even if subsequently you need to bring them gently down to earth.

If you have ever rushed into your boss's office with an idea so

151

great you had to tell them about it immediately and found yourself with the last, strangled 'Eureka!' dying in your throat as, without even looking up, they growled, 'I've no time to talk to you now', you will know just what it feels like to be dis-paced and how demotivating it can be.

If you don't pace people who come to you with ideas, they might not come to you with the next one – and that one could have been a world beater.

Don't forget that as manager you are the coach, the one who can slow down the other person's pace or speed it up to help you to talk things over as *adults*.

YOUR STAFF AND EGO STATES

Psychologists identify three main ego states which are revealed by people's voices, the words they use and their body language: the child ego; the parent ego; and the adult ego. You will learn to recognize which state is predominant by observing people as soon as they come into your office and by listening to the words they use. In fact they will be using words and phrases they have used over and over again in similar circumstances, based largely on their childhood experiences.

In the child ego state, people tend to say things like 'Listen! I'm not doing that. You're always trying to give me extra work!' ... 'If only you'd be more helpful'. ... 'You never see my point of view and if you insist on doing it that way I'm going straight to Mr Richards.'

The parent ego can be either controlling and restricting or caring and helpful. The controlling parent uses words like 'I've told you a hundred times' and 'This has got to stop', while the caring parent says things like 'It won't take me too long' or 'I'd like to help.'

In the adult ego state, people use expressions like 'What do you think?', 'What are our options?' or 'Why do you think that happened?'. In fact, they ask all of the 'W' questions. They want to 'define', to 'experiment', to 'find out' and to 'work out solutions'. They assure other people that they 'understand' them and realize why they are disappointed or upset.

Managers need to 'pace' people's voices, body language and the words they use until they are able to guide them towards the *adult* ego state. To do this they need to be aware of their own ego states and how they express them. Only then will they be able to act as a conversational role model.

SPEAKING AS ADULTS

To ensure that your conversations are encounters between *adults*:

- listen carefully to what the other person is saying;
- ask questions that give them a chance to 'open up': 'What more can you tell me about the Cassels situation, Barbara?';
- be specific. Ask the 'W' questions: 'Who, what, when exactly ...?';
- check the facts: 'Do we have all the latest data?'; 'Are these figures correct?';
- leave options open: 'We could see if there's another way to do this'; 'Why don't we look at the alternatives and get together tomorrow?';
- admit you are wrong if you have made a mistake: 'You are absolutely right, John. I don't know what I was thinking of.' – even if you later turn this to your advantage by 'stroking' and delegating. 'You really saved our bacon there, John. I think you'd better look after that side of things in future.'

EVERYONE WANTS SOMETHING

Managers soon learn that people rarely say exactly what they mean, either because they are unable to express themselves clearly, because they wish to conceal their real intentions or because they don't know what they want.

This makes many conversational situations difficult and, if they are to operate effectively, managers must be able to translate and decode other people's words. Of course, identifying ego states and reading body language will help but, on a day-to-day basis, a less complicated way of determining what people really mean is needed.

Fortunately there is a simple rule of thumb which can be applied to every communication and which is based on the assumption that *everyone* who opens their mouth to speak – or for that matter begins to write – *wants something*.

Of course, there is nothing intrinsically wrong in wanting things; it was wanting things that led human beings to communicate in the first place, and it is wanting things which motivates the world of the workplace.

In much the same way, there is nothing wrong about the fact that all human beings are egocentric and therefore consider what *they* want to be of prime importance.

Because of this it is possible to apply the everyone wants something rule to all conversations and to ask, without any cynical overtones, '*Cui bono*? – Who benefits?' or 'What's in it for them?' and 'What's in it for me in my capacity of manager?'

WORKPLACE CODES

Workplace codes and 'in' vocabulary usually show that your department is coming together and developing as a workplace family so that, unless they are being used to exclude others, they are usually a good sign.

They include nicknames and, provided it is neither cruel nor critical, if your staff have given you a nickname or a title it normally means that you have been accepted as 'the old man', or 'the boss', and will emphasize rather than detract from your authority.

DO YOU REMEMBER?

Do you remember things easily? Do members of your staff sometimes forget things of importance? Try planting mnemonics in your conversation – and in other communications – by using the 'association of ideas'.

Do you remember, for example, who it was who said, 'The reason we have two ears and only one mouth is that we need to listen more and talk less'? Of course, it was the Greek philosopher whose name occurs earlier in this chapter, and the reason that you stand a very good chance of remembering this particular piece of information is that we incorporated a mnemonic in the form of a reference to the Marx Brothers.

YOU ARE ALWAYS ON STAGE

The most important thing to remember is that, as a manager, you are always on stage and that the way in which you talk to people will provide a role model for the whole of your staff.

Begin as soon as you enter your workplace or even as you approach it, by saying a cheerful 'Good morning!' to everyone you meet, preferably greeting them by name and where possible with a positive remark.

You can do all this without even breaking your stride, and a 'Good morning, Fiona. Great job on the Davis business!' will increase Fiona's contribution to the day's work of your department by a considerable percentage.

Even the upbeat way in which you say 'Good morning' and the real concern in your voice as you ask 'Feeling better, John?' set the tone of the workplace as optimistic and caring.

THE CONTROL QUOTIENT

Most of the factors involved when talking to people and when coaching your staff to talk to people effectively are well within your *control*. You can set an example of *adult* conversation. You can coach people to improve the way they use words when talking to you, to each other and to your internal or external customers.

HOW WILL YOU KNOW YOU HAVE SUCCEEDED?

You will know that you and your staff are using verbal communication effectively when there are fewer, if any, rows and when people come to you with ideas and with problems because they know that they will be given a hearing.

At the same time, you will find productivity and quality

improving because staff are communicating well with each other and showing more respect for what other people want.

Your success will be confirmed beyond doubt when you and your staff begin saying such things as 'I'm sorry, I'm afraid I was wrong there' or 'Perhaps we could find a different answer'.

SUMMARY

- Why you could be wasting as much as two months a year if you are not using verbal communication skills effectively.
- How to cut out superfluous conversation and get the best out of the rest.
- The lost art of listening and how to apply the 80–20 Pareto Principle.
- How to achieve rapport by 'pacing' the person you are talking to. The dangers of 'dis-pacing'.
- How to detect ego states and to make sure that you and all the members of your department speak to each other as *adults*.
- The everyone wants something rule and its use in finding out what people really mean.
- How the words *you* use and the way you use them can improve the morale and productivity of your department from the time you step into your workplace.

FIFTEEN

A Few Moving Words

For many people there are few more frightening occasions in life than the moment when someone turns to them and says, 'Perhaps you would just say a few words'.

Of course, speaking to groups should be no more terrifying than speaking to individuals but, perhaps because of some atavistic fear of being outnumbered, it is something that many otherwise courageous men and women view with apprehension.

Fortunately most managers are made of sterner stuff because many of them spend a great deal of their working lives speaking in public, whether to meetings of half a dozen or so or to an assembled workforce of hundreds.

In fact, because of the synergetic effect of groups, speaking to more than two or three people can be a lot more effective than speaking to individuals. This makes it a vital skill for front-line managers who have to talk to their teams, to their staff, to their fellow-managers and perhaps to people outside their organization.

SMILE – YOU HAVE AN AUDIENCE

Ironically, in many ways speaking to groups is not only more effective than speaking to each individual separately, but is also easier because all groups of people, whether they have come together as a team, a meeting, a negotiating body, a seminar or a lecture group, are an audience. All that you, as a speaker, have to do is to learn how to 'work' them.

Any audience, from a team to a lecture hall full of people, rapidly becomes an entity and, while this may seem frightening at first, you can afford to 'act' to an audience by using larger gestures and more emotive words. Imagine yourself making a rousing political speech to just one person and you will appreciate the difference.

Getting groups on your side needs skill and experience, but the feeling that you are 'carrying them with you', whether they are buying a product or a project, is one of the joys of management.

HOW BEING A MANAGER HELPS

If you are one of those people who feels apprehensive at the thought of speaking to groups it is worth remembering that in most cases, if only because of your position, the 'audience' is unlikely to tear you to pieces.

Your own staff, for example, will almost certainly give you a polite hearing, as will groups of colleagues or senior managers who are keen to hear your contribution. It is up to you to capitalize on this by arousing and sustaining their interest and by achieving rapport with your 'audience', whether you are addressing one of your teams, a weekly production meeting or a promotions board.

THE 'W' QUESTIONS YET AGAIN

Unless you are caught on the hop and forced to improvise, you should ask the 'W' questions before speaking to any group. Ask yourself:

- *who* will constitute the group? Obviously you will need to assess individuals in the case of smaller groups, but in larger groups the 'who' is easier to determine as it is possible to establish a 'mean'. This often makes it easier to feel the pulse of a group of people than to sense the mood of one person;
- *what* do you need to say? The same sensitivity which enables speakers to sway groups of people makes audiences and crowds immediately aware of any lack of preparation on the

speaker's part. You must know exactly what you want to
say;

- *why* do you need to say anything at all? Is your meeting
  really necessary; and will it advance the cause of your
  organization?
- *where* is the venue? An important question, especially for
  public speakers;
- *when* will the group get together? Settling dates can be tricky.

MAKING MEETINGS EFFECTIVE

Meetings can be extremely useful and productive but, because
they tend to be more fun than other types of work, there is a
tendency to over-indulge in them.

One American management consultancy estimated that managers earning over £25,000 a year spend more than half their
time in meetings – and waste a lot of it in useless discussion and
office politics.

Check your own meetings and those of your staff for likely
cost-effectiveness. It may seem self-evident, but many managers
don't seem to appreciate that it is not worth holding a meeting
costing several thousand pounds in terms of participants' time
and interruption to other work in order to discuss the saving of
a few hundred pounds.

Hold stand-up meetings with no chairs in the room. Time
your meetings to end just before everyone is due to leave for
home, or put up a notice saying 'This meeting is costing £xxx
a minute'.

PLANNING, PREPARATION, PROCEDURE AND FOLLOW-UP

- *Planning*. Use the 'W' questions to determine: who should
  attend (as few as possible); the best time; the objectives; the
  topics to be discussed; your views regarding each topic;
  the venue; the agenda; availability of information.
- *Procedure*. Start punctually; follow the agenda; leave

potentially tricky problems till last; wind up by summing up conclusions reached.

- *Follow-up.* Get the note-taker to produce a report of the meeting including details of decisions made, actions required and by whom. Distribute to all concerned parties – not just participants.

Agendas are an important feature of meeting planning. Get them out to participants in good time. Schedule all points to be discussed and mark individual copies where necessary to indicate that the staff member concerned will be expected to make a major contribution.

Your *control* factor of meetings organized in this way is high. You can increase it by chairing the meeting or coaching the person selected to chair it to involve everyone, to make sure every point on the agenda is covered satisfactorily and to keep things moving.

Thank people for attending and, where appropriate, for a good and productive meeting. Set a time for the next meeting, even if all you say is, 'Thank you, ladies and gentlemen. See you all tomorrow, same time, same place'.

'MASTERMIND' MEETINGS

Create a 'Think Tank' of two or three colleagues whose problems are similar to your own. Define objectives, i.e. to solve specific problems on the basis that 'three or four heads are better than one'. Co-opt superiors, subordinates and specialists as temporary members, where appropriate. Approached in the right way, your colleagues will be pleased to take part and you – and they – will benefit from the knowledge and experience of several managers.

OTHER PEOPLE'S MEETINGS

- Try to attend only those you know will be productive: 'Sorry. I have another meeting scheduled for that time.'
- Be on time. Be prepared. Be brief.

- Observe the other people at the meeting for tell-tale body language and revealing ego-state vocabulary.
- Other people's meetings are a splendid opportunity to 'make your mark', but you must be sure of yourself and your facts as well as of your ability to put your case across interestingly and succinctly.

PUBLIC SPEAKING

As a front-line manager it is virtually certain that you will be called on to do some public speaking, if only at retirement functions, presentations and so on, but the occasions – and the opportunities – will increase as you move up in grade. This makes it an art worth learning now.

Take every chance to practise at family gatherings, sports clubs and even by telling jokes in your local pub. Use a tape recorder to practise your speeches.

The secret is to have confidence.

Experienced public speakers may make unplanned speeches but they never speak without planning. Take a leaf out of their book by preparing and committing to memory a couple of 'templates' of all-purpose speeches. Use delaying tactics, if necessary, to give yourself a few seconds to recall and mentally edit templates before starting.

For more formal occasions, make sure you have checked venue, time, subject, duration, name of audience group, names and titles of host and platform personalities. Write down names etc. on postcards. Check sound equipment and the like, even if it means arriving early.

Limit your pre-speech drinks to one weak one. Microphones make one drink sound like three and three like a bottle.

Aim for spontaneity. Don't read your speech, but prepare 'cues' on numbered postcards, using letters large enough to read while they are lying on the lectern or desk. You may not even need to use the cards. Merely knowing they are in your pocket will give you tremendous confidence.

Don't select one person in the audience to speak to. The person you choose will think they have a spot on their nose – at the very least – while everyone else will feel neglected. Instead, pick two or three people in different sections of the audience and allow your eyes to range over the whole group as you shift your regard from one to another.

Keep to time and query all requests to speak for longer than 10 to 15 minutes, plus time for questions. If anyone asks you to speak for longer, remind them that TV script writing is calculated at three words a second, which is 180 words a minute – 10,800 words or ten feature articles an hour.

Enquire if there are any people with trains or buses to catch and leave time for questions and a summing up, plus hosts' speeches. There's nothing like a mass exodus to ruin your evening.

SEMINARS

Seminars are organized occasions for conveying information to groups and are usually a great deal less formal than lectures. There is frequently an element of purposeful entertainment, which is why guest speakers often include sporting personalities.

Organization – covering all the 'W' questions – should be meticulous and it is often useful to have a preliminary get-together before the first session, making sure everyone has identifying badges. Create informal staff-led working teams which will remain together for discussion groups etc.

Supply delegates with PR fact sheets, publicity and – after the seminar – copies of speeches.

If you and your staff are organizing the seminar, aim for a touch of panache – IML for instance serve a champagne breakfast – and see that your staff are all smartly dressed to emphasize the importance of the occasion.

Make sure you get feedback, both on the spot and when the delegates have had a chance to digest the seminar material.

If your staff attend seminars, ask them for a written report covering pertinent material.

COACHING YOUR STAFF TO SPEAK TO GROUPS

If you intend to involve your staff fully in the work of your department and to benefit from their input, each of them must be able to speak with confidence, not merely to individuals but to groups.

Motivate them by pointing out that they will not be able to show themselves in the best light, to contribute to decisions which affect them, or to put forward their ideas unless they are able to speak to groups.

Begin by ensuring that all your staff make a contribution to team-working and identify the people with problems. Build up their confidence by telling them that their input will be valuable and single them out for encouragement. Make sure that neither you nor any of the rest of your staff make fun of them if they are slow or hesitant at first. Encourage them to practise with a tape recorder and to take any opportunity to speak outside the workplace, especially those which involve talking to a few friends or relatives. Make sure they realize that most public-speaking skills are interchangeable and that every time they speak to more than a couple of people they are gaining valuable experience. A tiny part in an amateur dramatics production, for example, could make all the difference to their performance when their audience is a promotions board.

Point out to those who are shy or who have minor speech impediments that many actors and TV personalities began successful careers precisely because of the efforts they made to overcome similar handicaps.

THE CONTROL QUOTIENT

Your degree of *control* over most of your speaking to groups will be high and in some cases, where you can decide such factors as participants, venue, times, agenda and so on, very high indeed.

As your newly articulate staff begin to exercise their abilities to talk to groups and to sway them, you may feel that you are losing a degree of control. In fact, you stand to gain by allowing them to realize their full potential in this way and, as manager, you retain sufficient control to be able to channel their efforts to the benefit of your department.

HOW WILL YOU KNOW YOU HAVE SUCCEEDED?

You will know that you are getting through to groups when you are able to make each occasion to speak to a number of people a 'performance' and sense that you are carrying your audiences with you.

You will feel that you are able to use most meetings – whatever the topic – to project energy and optimism.

Because of this, your efficiently organized meetings will not only be successful and productive, but also enjoyable, with every participant coming away feeling confident, refreshed and revitalized.

Meanwhile, coaching your staff to speak to groups effectively will vastly increase the productivity of your departmental teams and enable your people – on your behalf – to bring added influence to bear on any outside meetings they may attend.

SUMMARY

- Why front-line managers need to be able to speak to groups if they are to be effective in meetings, seminars and presentations. The advantages of speaking to groups.
- Why many people are apprehensive about speaking to more than one or two people and how these fears can be overcome.
- How to make your meetings effective by planning, preparation and procedure. Why following up meetings can make all the difference.
- Creating your own 'Think Tank' or how to recruit a team of managers to help you run your department.
- Public speaking: a useful skill for front-line managers and an essential one for those who intend to move up. How to make sure you never dry up. How to 'plan' off-the-cuff speeches.

- How to get the most out of seminars as an organizer, a delegate, or a delegate's manager.
- Why you should coach your staff to speak effectively in meetings.

SIXTEEN

Putting it in Writing

Managers need to be able to write clearly and concisely if they are to communicate with their staff, colleagues and superiors in such a way as to avoid mistakes and misunderstandings. They need to be able to issue instructions, to make reports and to have a record of what was said in case of dispute.

They must also be able to set down ideas and proposals for presentation to busy individuals whose attention has to be caught and held if they are to be persuaded to act.

As a manager you will need to write memos and letters to members of your staff, not only to give them instructions but also to motivate, to encourage and perhaps even to chide. Your written words are now more meaningful than when you were a member of the rank and file, which means that you have to take extra care that there is no possibility of their being misinterpreted.

THE TRAPS OF 'OFFICIALESE'

The manager's need to communicate in writing is complicated by the fact that many people believe that they can make their writing more impressive and effective by using pompous and convoluted language.

In fact, this view is so prevalent that some countries have recognized 'languages' for the Civil Service and business.

In English, 'officialese' remains unofficial, but there are still many managers in both the public and private sectors whose letters are masterpieces of obfuscation. Like stage police officers, they do not 'go' but 'proceed in the direction of', do not 'lay on a car' but 'arrange for suitable vehicular transport to be available as required'. Worse still, their anxiety to impress often leads them to write precisely the opposite of what they intend.

FEEL THE QUALITY – NOT THE LENGTH

Often the same people who go in for officialese and sesquipedalianism – the appropriate word for the obsessive use of long words – are also prone to write discursive letters containing sentences of Gothic length and obscurity. Writing such letters is not only asking for errors and misunderstandings but is also extremely time-consuming.

Some experts advise managers to save time by not aiming for perfection. It is much better to aim for as good a letter as possible and to save time by cutting down the length and the number of letters you write, and by keeping every communication as simple as possible. One way of making your ideas readily understandable is to imagine that you are writing in a foreign language. You would almost certainly marshal your ideas and simplify them before starting to write, in order to make things easier for both yourself and the recipient.

KEEP IT CRISP – KEEP IT SIMPLE!

Begin by asking yourself if you need to write at all or if a quick 'phone call might not do the job as well, if not better.

If you do decide to write, deal, wherever possible, with only one major topic per letter.

Assume that the person you are writing to has the attention span of a harassed grasshopper. They will almost certainly be busy and you will not be insulting them by making your letter easy to read.

Keep your letters short. Try to keep to one page if possible. It makes life easier for the reader and is an excellent discipline which forces writers to ask themselves what they really want to say. Sentences need not be telegraphic, but should be short enough to ensure that the grammar does not go awry and that the reader does not have to play 'hunt the verb'. Aim for a natural style, which usually means free of pedantry, even when the more complicated form is grammatically correct.

PROFESSIONAL ECONOMY

George Bernard Shaw, who recommended that writers should get down on paper at least two thousand words a day in order 'to professionalize themselves', could be economical with his own words.

To a landlord who was chivvying him to leave the house he was renting he wrote: 'Dear Sir, I remain, Yours faithfully, George Bernard Shaw.'

Not only short and to the point but memorable.

WRITE AS YOU SPEAK

Once you have planned your letter, decide on its content and give it form by noting down your ideas for a beginning, a middle and an end. It's often best to visualize the person you are writing to and to visualize their reactions as they read what you have written.

Then write a first draft using exactly the same language you would use if you were talking to them face to face. In this way you will achieve an effect of spontaneity, while striking exactly the right note of formality or informality you need to suit the person and circumstances. Check and amend the first draft, especially any names and facts, before sending the final version. In the case of very important letters it is often best, if there is time, to wait a couple of hours – and sometimes even overnight – before checking and sending out the final letter.

PERSONAL ADVERTISING

Managers should use letters not only to communicate facts but to project their personality.

Regard every letter as an opportunity to inspire, to motivate or to convince. Accentuate the positive by eliminating where possible any words which suggest doubt or lack of confidence.

Good manners will usually be all you need to dictate your correspondence style – and frequently the content too. If in any doubt, 'promote' the recipient.

Send – and persuade your staff to send – short notes of thanks for even the smallest 'above the call of duty' service and congratulations for every job well done, both in the department and outside it. Such notes are often treasured by the recipient and have an effect on morale which well repays the effort.

DRAFTING REPORTS

Writing reports is an important part of the front-line manager's duties and is frequently more effective than oral reporting as the recipient has more time to consider and analyse the communication.

However, if you are able, ask yourself if a particular report has value and query the need for periodic reports that have 'always' been made to or by your predecessor. Ask yourself whether such regular reporting is not inhibiting the reporting of events your superior needs to know about immediately.

Query the value of report forms. There is often a tendency to change the date and shuffle the data while reporting the same things week after week. Standard report forms can also prevent you from presenting things in order of priority.

KNOW YOUR RECIPIENT

When reporting to people you know well, and who know the subject well, it is often possible to use a telegraphic style. However, difficulties sometimes arise when you are not well acquainted with the recipient, or if there is more than one, each of whom requires a different level of detail and explanation if they are not to be either baffled or bored.

One solution is to provide a bullet point summary, followed if necessary by an examination of each point.

Break the report down into clearly defined elements and arrange these in order of priority.

DECIDE ON YOUR OBJECTIVES

If you report regularly, or someone asks for a lengthy report, get together to decide on the objectives of the report and agree them.

Do they, for example, require 'exception' reporting, i.e. that you report only when things are going exceptionally well or exceptionally badly? Front-line managers are rarely required to report purely historical information.

REPORTING BAD NEWS

We know some managers who would have been quite capable of submitting a detailed report to the captain of the *Titanic* telling him how well the band was playing and forgetting all mention of iceberg damage.

Not only is it inexcusable not to report bad news as well as good, but written reports are frequently the best way of conveying bad news as they give the recipient the facts and time to consider them unemotionally.

Insist that your staff report bad news in time for you to do something about it.

WORTH A THOUSAND WORDS

Use graphics if they will help make your point. As front-line manager you may not have control but there will usually be nothing to stop you saying, 'I've done the report in the usual way but I've included some separate graphics I think will be helpful'.

Thinking clearly about your reports may help you to marshal your ideas on the work of your department but you should not, like some new managers, fall into the trap of allowing the fact that you have to report to inhibit your actions.

If you are spending more time writing reports than on working, or if writing reports means you take work home more than two nights a week, you have a communication problem.

Substituting pictures for a few thousand words might help.

WINDOWS OF OPPORTUNITY

Cutting down the number of reports and retaining only those which are cost-effective, while slimming down those that remain by cutting out unnecessary verbiage, will make report writing less of a chore. You can then begin to view reports, not as time-consuming irrelevancies, but as 'windows of opportunity' for your staff, your company – and yourself.

Use your report-writing skills, for example, to put forward the results of your brainstorming sessions in the form of concrete proposals. Make your reports so interesting and informative, and your style so individual, that they stand a good chance of reaching senior management levels – unedited.

This is good personal PR and could increase your influence, but you should resist the temptation to use reports for organizational politics, if only because the fact that you were doing so would soon become obvious.

DELEGATING REPORTS

Report writing can be a useful field in which to delegate, provided you have coached those members of your staff who submit reports to you.

Your staff may at first find it more difficult to write reports than you did, but if you show them how to simplify their writing and how to present 'the news' – good or bad – they will soon become aware of the opportunities report writing provides to influence the affairs of the department and perhaps the company.

FIRING PEOPLE

The great fear of many new front-line managers is that they may have to fire people, perhaps even someone who is, or was, a friend.

It's a rotten job, but your writing skills may help to soften the blow by leaving the person concerned with their self-respect intact. Provided the reason for dismissal is not dishonesty, it can be attributed to 'restructuring' or 'the need for a different combination of talents'.

The person concerned might 'do better with another company'. Be well mannered. We remember one senior executive who first learned he'd been fired when his successor announced coldly, 'Your presence at this meeting is no longer required', and who bounced back a month or two later as boss of the company. No prizes for guessing the first thing he did on his return.

KEEP IT TIGHT, KEEP IT SIMPLE – BUT KEEP IT INTERESTING

Once you and your staff have made all your letters, memos and reports simple, short and informative you can concentrate on making them memorable.

Use shock tactics or tricks like changing the words of clichés and proverbs. Employ alliteration's artful aid, humour, or even rhyme if you think it will make your message stick.

Memorable words can be surprisingly effective. We knew one national newspaper journalist who for many years kept a note from his editor criticising his expenses, simply because of its scathing humour and the way in which it was written.

In fact, the reporter in question was so impressed that he showed the tattered memo to his fellow-journalists at every opportunity, which, if it made their expenses claims only slightly less imaginative, must have saved the paper many thousands of pounds.

COMMUNICATING WITH GROUPS – PUBLIC RELATIONS

You may think, especially if your organization has a high-powered public relations department, that exterior public relations is one area which need not concern you overmuch. In fact, there is frequently a lot that front-line managers can do to improve the image of their department.

If you have outside customers it is obvious that everything you do to increase the quality of your goods or the services you provide will be good for your department's image, and you should do your best to get the maximum effect from your work and from your success by publicizing them. Liaise with your PR Department, if you have one, by telling them of any triumphs you think people should know about as soon as they happen. These may be workplace successes or sporting victories, either by individuals or teams. The main thing is to get the news out while it is still news.

Feed your PR people, the local paper or your local news agency with lots of short items. They can always come back for more details if they need them. If you have no PR department you should clear activity of this sort with your boss. Write sparely, remember the five Ws: Who? What? Why? Where? When? – and get the most interesting point into the first paragraph. Getting some free publicity for the company in this way will do your own image no harm and it will be good training for dealing with the press at a later stage in your career.

INTERNAL PUBLIC RELATIONS

Internal PR is frequently neglected by front-line managers who should make full use of every in-house opportunity to boost their staff and their department.

Use notice boards, posters, circulars, house newspapers and magazines, electronic mail and in-house videos where available to bring the good work of your staff to the attention of everyone in the organization. It will do wonders for your staff morale.

No need to mention your name if you don't wish to. Some of the credit for your department's workplace successes, or their victories at football or Scrabble, is bound to rub off.

NEWSLETTERS – A FRONT-LINE INITIATIVE

There are two main types of newsletter. One 'motivational', usually professionally produced on behalf of senior management and aimed at motivating and informing staff. They often have the feel of a glossy magazine and, as they frequently have better format than copy, they are a good outlet for the PR-conscious front-line manager.

By contrast, 'service' newsletters – although funded by employers – are written by and for employees and often enjoy a high degree of autonomy. They contain staff news and gossip, but also news from teamwork groups and news of workplace problems and successes. Because they can be produced with the help of equipment available in most modern offices, the cost of such newsletters is not high. They provide excellent practice in teamworking, a useful forum for airing all topics of interest to the producing group and often a 'guest spot' for the departmental manager.

As the 'local rags' of the workplace they make a good front-line management initiative.

Newsletters can be used to back up other PR initiatives like departmental sports teams and charity projects which can help weld your department into a well-motivated team.

STAFF PARTICIPATION

You might want to delegate the PR job to one of your staff or let them take it in turns to write reports for the company's in-house magazine.

You could also set up a team to create and run a departmental news sheet which would, among other things, open up a new communication medium between you and your staff.

THE CONTROL QUOTIENT

You can *control* most of the factors and *influence* many of the others, so your control quotient is high. If your boss is one of those people who feels the width of reports rather than the quality, you may have to convince them that cutting down will be in their interests, but otherwise you should be able to coach your staff to write well and keep control by, say, holding a 'letter of the week' competition for the most effective written communication.

HOW WILL YOU KNOW YOU HAVE SUCCEEDED?

You will know you are on the right track when you begin to get interesting reports from your staff, giving you all the information you need, and so well written that you feel tempted to quote extracts from them outside the workplace.

Another good sign is when few if any letters sent out by your staff result in requests for clarification, but the real accolade comes when someone 'phones you to say, 'I had a note from one of your people this morning. I'd never seen things put as well as that. It really made me think'.

SUMMARY

- Why you need to be able to write clearly and concisely, not just to manage the day-to-day running of your department but to present ideas and projects.
- Avoiding errors and misunderstandings by banning long words, flowery phrases and 'officialese'.
- How good manners dictate style and why you should, if possible, wait before checking first drafts and before sending off the finished communication.
- Getting the most from reports by eliminating unnecessary ones, being aware of what the recipient really wants to know, and by regarding every report you write, not as a chore, but as a 'window of opportunity'.
- Why you should report the bad news along with the good – and do so quickly.
- When a picture really can be worth a thousand words.
- Coaching your staff to write well. Once they are submitting clear and concise reports to you, you can delegate some of your report writing to them as a motivating responsibility – and opportunity.
- Interior and exterior public relations.

SEVENTEEN

Managing the Electronic Office

As a new manager you almost certainly belong to an age group which is computer-literate and accustomed to using advanced technology, if only in the home.

This is fortunate because in many cases you will be using sophisticated equipment which your predecessor of only a few years ago would have regarded as pure science fiction. Technology is moving so rapidly that even the most advanced equipment can be superseded in a matter of months.

This usually makes it advisable to play yourself in before investing in new equipment and you may even find that you take over a department in which the current equipment is not being used to the full, often because the former manager was resistant to new technology.

YOU DON'T HAVE TO SPEND A FORTUNE

Equipment need not be overly sophisticated or expensive to be effective. One example of this is the cassette recorder which you and your staff can use to good effect in the office, in meetings, at conferences, on planes or trains or when travelling by car.

With a recorder costing less than a hundred pounds you have the services of a 'secretary' for 24 hours a day, enabling you to dictate letters and memos, to make notes of meetings and to jot down ideas as they occur to you.

Recording 'phone conversations, especially if you use a stop watch to 'flag' appropriate sections of tape, gives you a permanant record and allows you to play back interesting points to determine not only what the speaker said but how they said it.

Cassette recorders can also be used for training purposes, to increase verbal skills, to coach employees or to 'teach' specific subjects.

TELEPHONE PLUS

If your office 'phones offer more than the basic facilities it could be worth while checking to see if your staff – especially the older people – are making full use of them. You could find for instance that they are making no use of things like recall buttons and automatic dialling, and that a couple of minutes' coaching would make them a great deal more effective.

You might also decide that adding an answering machine to some of your workstations, especially those of people who have to move around either inside or outside the workplace, would increase the efficiency of your department at relatively low cost. You could consider pagers and mobile 'phones. Remind people who have answering machines that their recorded message may be a customer's important first contact with your department.

FAX MACHINES, PHOTOCOPIERS AND CALCULATORS

Fax machines and photocopiers are now such an integral part of most office set-ups that it is easy to forget that people sometimes need training in their use. Make sure that new staff especially are taught how to use the machines correctly: 'You'll soon get the hang of it' is not usually adequate.

If you are not already using fax for internal use, make your own feasibility study. It could help to speed up the work of your department.

Make sure that everyone who needs a pocket calculator has one and knows how to use it. We know one otherwise highly efficient and superbly equipped garage where mechanics spend more time working on customers' bills than they do on their cars. A calculator costing two or three pounds would save customers having to wait and free highly trained staff to do charge-able work.

Use brainstorming sessions to generate ideas for making use of existing equipment, both large and small, before considering more expensive purchases like computers.

COMPUTER POWER

Computers make many of today's front-line managers more powerful than their predecessors. A tiny desk-top model, for example, has the calculating ability of tens if not hundreds of pen-pushing clerks and, at the touch of a key, can find infor-mation which once had to be tracked down in a roomful of files.

Not so long ago computers were the prerogative of large organ-izations able to afford computer rooms filled with machines the size of fridge-freezers.

Today, even quite small businesses have some kind of com-puter, either for accounting at basic level or for wordprocessing. If they have stores, or manufacturing capability, it is virtually certain that a number of the processes will have been computer-ized, which means that many younger managers will have used computers before being promoted.

COMPUTER LITERACY

Even if you are not already accustomed to using computers in the workplace, you may have used them for game playing, while many of the machines themselves have become more 'user friendly'.

You may be more computer literate than you think but, even if you have used computers in the workplace, you will probably have done so in a 'passive' role. You will not have been respons-ible for deciding whether they should be used for any given process, but will usually have accepted current procedure as part of the job.

As a front-line manager you need to be able to think of com-puters more actively and to decide for instance whether the procedures your staff are using are appropriate.

Instead of merely putting things up on screen and accepting that the computer system does what it does, you should now take the initiative and say, if necessary, 'The current computer system is all very well but it doesn't fit the bill as far as I'm concerned.' This is the equivalent of a front-line manager of pre-computer days saying, 'I don't want you to record information on paper in that way. In future I'd like you to do it this way.'

Of course, you may not be able to make radical changes yourself but you should be prepared to ask, for example, whether the computer could be employed in an area in which it is not already being used.

THE DIY MANAGER

In pre-computer days record-keeping was almost always the secretary's job and managers were not expected to be involved, but nowadays most managers have at least one computer on their desk and input information as they become aware of it. In fact, as computers become cheaper, even very small organizations – and small departments of large companies – have computers junior managers can use.

For instance, managers at all levels would once have used a secretary if they wanted to get a report typed, but now anyone who can type with two fingers can use a word processor to present reports and letters. Again, if a secretary is asked to prepare a document, the manager can amend it without the need for complete retyping.

This can save a lot of stress, especially for new managers, some of whom were once intimidated by their secretaries to the point where they would let letters go out with a few hand-written corrections rather than ask for them to be retyped.

OFFICE ADMINISTRATION

As computers become available to lower grades, they are being used more and more for office administration functions as well as for data processing.

Computer diary systems can be helpful and you may, for

instance, have a communal diary which you can use to find out whether people will be available at any given time. This makes it possible for secretaries to arrange meetings for a number of people, an exercise which once entailed a great deal of checking, 'phoning and running about.

ELECTRONIC MAIL

In many larger organizations office automation takes the word processing procedure a stage further and companies, instead of producing hard copy documents for distribution throughout the organization, use electronic mail, the advantages of which include:

- a dramatic reduction in the amount of 'bumf' floating round the organization;
- 'recorded delivery' – the system records the fact that documents have been looked at;
- a hard copy option for recipients, who can print out from their own terminal if they wish;
- the facility for keeping material on file;
- the ease with which documents can be worked on or amended;

By using electronic mail you can transmit documents much as you would when using a fax machine; the difference is that the information is 'processable'. This means that companies can have an 'electronic typing pool' to prepare documents to send out to any point in the organization, where the local staff can make their own contribution.

There are many other facets of office automation and the hardware changes constantly. For example, a couple of years ago you might have had a fax machine and a word processor, plus a computer for doing the accounts, stock control and so on.

Today, the hardware is interchangeable and you are more likely to find that you have one machine for photocopying, writing, printing and storing documents, as well as receiving fax – and it's still small enough to go on top of your desk!

THE NEW MANAGER AND THE STATUS QUO

It is usually prudent for new managers to accept the status quo until they have found their feet, but too many of them, especially where computer systems are concerned, go on doing things in the same way as their predecessor.

As a manager you need to be 'pro-active' as far as computers are concerned and this means being constantly on the look-out for new ways to use them.

This doesn't mean that you have to persuade your company to spend large sums of money on new hardware. Your current computer may well have capabilities that are not being used, in which case you may be able to increase the efficiency of your department simply by reading the manual or investing in some relatively inexpensive additional software.

As a new manager you are in the best possible position to know how any given system *does not* work and to make suggestions for improvement.

By contrast, your senior managers may not know how the system works at all. They may well have been involved in the decision to buy the system but they will almost certainly have had little if anything to do with its day-to-day operation.

YOUTH ON YOUR SIDE

You could well have youth on your side compared to the older members of your organization who may still be resistant to the use of computers. Such resistance is almost always a matter of age and many older managers of computer companies are as reluctant to use computers to manage their own affairs as their contemporaries in other types of business.

Of course, reluctance to enlarge and improve computer systems may not be due only to the age of the senior managers. The age of the company may have a lot to do with it. In many cases, large and long-established firms are at a disadvantage because, as pioneers, they invested heavily in hardware which is now, if not obsolete, rather long in the tooth and which they cannot afford to change.

181

If your company is relatively young and small it will have been able to start off with current technology fairly cheaply and may never have the same problems as the pioneers, as the trend is towards software which will enable computers of different generations to talk to each other.

SECURITY

Computers enable many people to have access to the same information but in a well-set up system it is possible to store confidential information more securely than in a filing cabinet.

The usual procedure is to restrict such information to the user and their immediate superior. If there is any material that you do not wish your superior to see, either for 'tactical' reasons or because their doing so might breach the confidence of someone who reports to you, the best thing is to keep the disc in question at home.

PORTABLE POWER

There was a time when managers took work home with them. Now they are more likely to take the office home with them, as many organizations have invested in portable computers that are smaller than portable typewriters.

The input to these machines can be fed into the larger computers at the office or the two machines can be linked by modem. In this way managers can access and process an enormous amount of information while they are travelling or at home.

THE FRIENDLY REVOLUTION

Fortunately, if paradoxically, sophisticated technology has made most electronic devices easier to use and the days when the fax machine could only be operated by an official appointee are long gone.

Computers are now increasingly 'user friendly', with sophisticated software which guards against the pitfalls beginners might otherwise encounter. You and your staff will find it easier to use them than did your predecessors, but the time-hallowed advice to 'Read the ******* manual!' remains valid.

Read the manual yourself – even if you are already an expert on computers of different makes – and coach your staff to do so.

Set up a procedure which requires your computer-users to 'save' at specific appropriate intervals and to 'copy' discs and individual documents, even if hard copy already exists. Unfortunately, like most computer-users – including someone not a million miles away from this PC – you will never know how important this is until you or your staff have 'lost' an appreciable amount of work.

PUT PEOPLE FIRST

Managers should be careful not to buy sledgehammer computers to crack information nuts or to hide behind computers when a face-to-face meeting would be better. Don't become a computer 'junkie'.

Computers can distance you from the human side of management, so it is as well to remind yourself every now and again that the information churned out by your machines is prepared by real people and refers to real people and their requirements.

THE CONTROL QUOTIENT

New managers will usually find that they have a high degree of *control* over the way in which their department's current technology is used and it is here that time invested in coaching is likely to pay immediate dividends.

Once your department is using technology effectively, you should also be able to influence new purchases and to make sure that any equipment acquired is cost-effective.

HOW WILL YOU KNOW YOU HAVE SUCCEEDED?

You will know you are succeeding when employees begin to say things like 'I didn't know it could do that' and make suggestions for optimizing the use of current equipment, or begin campaigning for goodies they have read about in computer magazines.

There should also be a decrease in computer foul-ups and an increase in efficiency and productivity.

SUMMARY

- Electronic equipment that can improve the work of your department without costing a fortune. The small machines that can make a difference while you are still playing yourself in.
- Coaching your staff to make the optimum use of the technology they already have.
- Computer power, computer literacy and the advantages of being a young person in a young company.
- The DIY manager and office administration. Using computer diaries and electronic mail.
- The 'user-friendly' computer and why you and your staff should still read the manual and 'save' information to save your sanity.
- Crunch numbers, not people! Even in the computer age management is still a people business.

EIGHTEEN

Asking and Negotiating

Many new managers worry about their ability to get people to do as they wish, because they know that giving instructions to staff is one of the fundamental duties of management.

In fact, the easiest way to get people to do what you want them to do is often to ask them to do it. This is even more effective for managers who, when speaking to their staff, benefit from their authority and from the implied contract that, in return for being paid, employees will do as they ask.

However, managers who ask incorrectly will find their staff reluctant to comply and their colleagues and superiors adamant. This is usually because they have not moved on much further than infantile pointing and demanding, but lack the child's ability to accompany its demands with a dimpled smile. Instead, they either ask brusquely or shilly-shally so that the people they are asking to do things end up feeling offended or impatient.

HOW TO ASK

Fortunately, asking correctly is an art which first-line managers can learn themselves and teach to their staff – beginning with the use of expressions like 'please', 'would you mind?' and 'I wonder if you could help me?'

These words have a near-magical effect, especially if you back them up by:

- knowing exactly what you want people to do. Not knowing this can lead to the sort of stammering and stuttering that makes it easy for people – especially bosses, colleagues and clients – to say no. Write down what you want from people, especially if you are going to ask them on the 'phone;

- asking the right people. Make sure that, if possible, you know who you need to ask before you begin and that you have their correct name and title. Check these with secretaries where possible and try to find out if their boss is the right person to ask.

    If you ask the wrong colleague, superior or outsider for something, they may simply refuse. If you ask the wrong employee, they may try to comply, rather than put you right, with perhaps disastrous results.

    If you don't know who you need to ask to do something, ask for information;

- putting a good case. If your request is a simple one, make it brief to avoid talking yourself out of a satisfactory reply.

    If your request is tricky or complicated, write down the headings of your case on post cards – especially if you are asking on the 'phone – to enable you to deal with hesitancy or a refusal;

- offering a quid pro quo. If doing as you wish will help the other person in the long run, tell them 'what's in it' for them, before they ask. Keep a little something in reserve just in case;

- using polite persistence. Polite persistence pays. If you get a refusal, keep on asking, without irritation, and varying your words and your tone with each request;

- asking with smiles, body language and humour. Use all your charm and communication skills, especially if asking on the 'phone. Rehearse your request, either mentally or using a tape recorder, until asking for things becomes almost second nature;

- having the right attitude. Request and invite rather than demand – even if you are in a position to insist on compliance. Save the big guns of direct orders for when they are really needed. That way you stand a chance of people saying things like, 'If we do as you ask, I think there's a chance that the building may catch fire', rather than 'We did as you ordered, and the building's on fire'.

- showing respect for the people you ask. Asking is one use of words which reveals disdain and contempt quicker than almost any other. Even if, at the moment, you are asking a subordinate to do something they cannot refuse to do, you may one day wish to ask them a real favour;
- using 'us' and 'we'. Make it clear that you are asking for a personal favour or service but, if you are asking for something which will also benefit the whole department, point this out;
- making asking a habit. Ask correctly for a lot of small things and compliance becomes a habit. This is a legitimate way of getting people to do as you wish, but its overuse, especially with colleagues, savours of manipulation. Make sure you know when people are trying to use it on *you*, so that you know exactly when to say no. Beware of colleagues who ask for small favours too frequently; they could be softening you up for the kill;
- building up credit. Favours are to some extent bankable so, while keeping a careful eye open for manipulators and exploiters, practise saying yes whenever possible to people who ask you for things;
- assuming compliance. Ask in such a way as to make it clear that you expect agreement and you will stand a very good chance of getting what you expect.

THE 'SELF-CONFIDENCE TRICK'

This certainty that people are going to do what you ask of them is one of the most important managerial attributes. It is almost totally a matter of self-confidence and, while it helps to have great wealth or power, these are not strictly necessary. In fact, getting people to do as you ask without having money or power is a 'confidence trick' without criminal intent.

If you have any doubts as to what people will do when asked by someone who expects compliance, you have only to watch one of those TV shows in which ordinary people do the most outrageous things simply because they are reluctant to say no to someone who patently expects them to say yes.

Practise outside the workplace by asking people to do things you know they will be reluctant to do, like serving a round of drinks after they have called 'Time!' or making you the exception to some pettifogging rule. Practise on family, friends, shop-keepers, hotel staff and civil servants until you have mastered a polite but utterly confident manner. In time you will become so accustomed to people doing as you ask that you will be genuinely astounded when someone refuses.

Back in the workplace, the knack of asking in this way will, with experience, become an easy habit of command and a firm conviction that colleagues and superiors will be glad to do as you wish. You will have acquired the magic wand of management.

LET'S NEGOTIATE

Everyone wants something. However, not everyone's wants are compatible and the primitive response to any situation in which two parties have different interests is to fight or flee.

Civilized people usually prefer to negotiate rather than fight or run away, but unfortunately some of them seem unable to shed the adversarial approach which makes much so-called nego-tiation a sort of disguised warfare.

In the workplace where much – though not all – negotiation takes place between employees and management, this adversarial approach, which presupposes that there must be 'winners' and 'losers', only emphasizes any existing 'them' and 'us' attitudes and makes real agreement impossible.

Genuine negotiation is a means of co-ordinating interests and resolving difficulties peacefully, by aiming for a 'win-win' situ-ation which allows for gain on both sides.

PREPARING TO NEGOTIATE

Preparation is essential for any successful negotiation and should include:

- determining exactly what is being negotiated. What does the other side want? They are bound to want something, even if it is only to give the impression that they are willing to negotiate, to make a show of intransigence or to maintain the status quo. If they are not playing to the gallery, what will they be asking for?

- picking the home team. Select a balanced team of people who are experienced negotiators and whose background is relevant to the negotiations in hand;
- finding out about the opposite team. Its composition could affect the selection of the home team. Think of them as 'opposites' rather than opponents and, unless you already know them well, find out as much as you can about the individual members. Think of yourselves as negotiating not so much with the delegation from the Confederation of Whistle Blowers as with Freda Smith, Eric Jones, Christine Armthwaite and so on. Asking for the names and positions of negotiators is accepted practice. Follow it up by researching their background and character. It could be disconcerting to discover in the middle of negotiations that Freda – who looks like a barmaid – has a doctorate in religious studies, or that Eric's favourite ploy is to pretend to lose his cool;
- determining your opposites' mandate. This is a tough one, but there is nothing much worse than discovering that your opposites don't have the authority to make the concessions you have decided to press for. You could also find yourself confronted by unscrupulous negotiators who announce that what you have agreed is not covered by their mandate and that they will have to refer to their superiors;
- arranging the venue. This is more important than one might think, as are all the other physical details of the meeting, like having the right size and shape of table, laying on refreshments where appropriate and making sure that there are suitable lavatories, if both male and female delegates are expected. It is winning tactics to make the visiting team as comfortable as possible;
- having all the necessary facts and figures to hand. You could have a computer terminal in the room but it would be polite to ask your opposites if they agree.

189

THE PRE-NEGOTIATION CAUCUS

A caucus is a useful word employed by negotiators to describe a closed meeting of either side in a negotiation.

It is often called in the course of negotiations – almost always with the consent of the opposite side – in order to analyse proposals and discuss tactics, in which case members can 'go into a huddle' without leaving the room.

The pre-negotiation caucus is used to decide what the opposite team really want and, more important, what they might be persuaded to settle for. It is at this stage – and not during negotiations – that your own team should settle any differences about aims and strategy.

You should also decide on specific 'roles' like 'good cop, bad cop'. At this stage, remember that a plan is just a plan and that, while it is essential to determine in advance your aims and what concessions you are prepared to make, flexibility is the keynote of successful negotiation.

'THEY' ARE NOT THE ENEMY

A pre-negotiation get-together, to introduce people and enable them to get to know their opposites, can also help to reduce any adversarial tension. Moving into another room or sitting down at the table is a convenient signal that formal negotiations have begun. It is not a declaration of war.

Now, in addition to making it clear that you regard your opposites as potential allies rather than enemies, you must yourself refuse to be pushed into the role of 'enemy'. This is the time for sweet reasonableness and friendly questions.

It is also the time to establish who is the real decision-maker among your opposites, who may not necessarily be the person designated as the head of the visiting team. Look for the person to whom the others defer, especially if they have the look of an unemotional observer. You will do a better job of convincing if you know who it is that you have to convince.

OPEN WITH A BANG

Being polite does not mean that you have to be mealy mouthed and it is often a good idea to open with a verbal right hook to make sure you have your opposites' attention.

A typical attention-getter of this sort is to make the most outrageous demand you could dream of getting away with, knowing that you will be happy to settle for much less. Now almost a cliché gambit, this has the additional effect of making your final settlement look better and easier to accept.

Follow your demand with a firm 'However,' and launch into an assurance of your willingness to negotiate. Your underlying theme should be 'We know what we want and we have an idea what you want. We'd like you to clarify what it is that you want so that together we can work out an agreement which will benefit everyone.'

YOU MAY NOT BE KING OF THE CASTLE

As a manager you should avoid any suggestion of arrogance. Lack of respect for your opposites is a sure way to lose any chance of agreement. You may feel that your team hold the high ground but it would be wrong to make this apparent. Imply that you are all negotiators and 'game players' whose aim is to leave the table feeling not only that you have concluded a satisfactory win-win agreement but that you are better friends than when you started.

Winning negotiators give the impression that they are anxious to say yes, and when their opposites ask 'What's in it for us?' they are prepared to reply, 'Well, let's look at that, shall we? We can probably work something out'.

'We', in fact, is the magic word which can transform two negotiating teams into one team in search of a solution.

SEEKING ALLIES AND BREAKING CODES

Negotiations can be fun and should always be exciting. You can't convince someone who is fast asleep so you should employ all your communication skills to make sure you retain the interest of the whole table.

Look for allies. A female negotiator, for example, might turn a woman opposite into an ally by merely raising an eyebrow when a male delegate says something which could be viewed as sexist.

Interpret codes, especially the language that hides a hidden meaning and can often be countered by a puzzled request for clarification. Look for body language give-aways and deliberate signals and watch yourself – especially if you negotiate frequently with the same people – for any unconscious habits which could betray what you are thinking.

DON'T FORGET TO ASK

Don't get so carried away by the cut and thrust of negotiation that you forget to ask, fairly early in the course of negotiations, for what you really want, and to ask for it several times, making absolutely clear what you are prepared to concede in exchange. Otherwise, you could find your opposite saying, at the end of a lengthy session, 'We didn't know you wanted X. We would have been prepared to concede a little less than X but we thought all along that what you wanted was Y and we weren't having that at any price.' In negotiating, whether you are a captain of industry or a schoolboy, 'if you don't ask, you don't get'.

THE CONTROL QUOTIENT

Your *control* quotient over the way you ask for things is high and, once you master the art, you can control the ways in which you coach your staff to use correct asking in their dealings with internal and external customers.

In negotiation, as front-line manager, you probably control many more factors than you think because it will usually be you who will determine things like the venue, the timetable and the composition of the 'home' team.

HOW WILL YOU KNOW YOU HAVE SUCCEEDED?

You will know that you are asking correctly when almost everyone does what you ask most of the time and when asking with the underlying assumption that people will comply becomes second nature.

You will know that you have coached your staff to ask for things correctly when you think to yourself, after one of them has left your office, 'However did they get me to agree to that?'

As for negotiating, there is no mistaking the satisfaction that comes from having made a deal, struck a bargain or reached an agreement which enables both sides to feel that they have won. The best negotiations finish up as celebrations.

SUMMARY

- Asking – the lost art of persuading people to do as you wish.
- How to ask correctly. Knowing what you want to ask and who you need to ask, and why asking incorrectly can lead to an almost inevitable refusal.
- Assuming compliance – the confidence which makes you genuinely surprised if someone refuses your request.
- Negotiation. Everyone wants something. If two parties want different things the choice is to fight, flee – or negotiate.
- Preparing to negotiate. Know your potential 'ally'. Choosing and briefing the home teams. The caucus, and why you should take time out for this official 'huddle'.
- Avoiding arrogance. Look for allies among your opposites and introduce 'we' to make everyone round the table a team with similar objectives.
- Why you need to ask, even when you are negotiating.

NINETEEN

Difficult Situations and Difficult People

Life for the front-line manager is rarely boring because, no matter how well you organize your department, there will always be the occasional crisis and the odd difficult person to provide a stimulating challenge. Well, that's one way of looking at it!

Fortunately, some fine-tuning of your day-to-day management methods will enable you to cope with most difficult situations, while your people skills, like motivation, will need only some slight adaptation when dealing with difficult people – who are often people with difficulties.

Regarding both difficult situations and difficult people as problems to be overcome, rather than crises, may make it possible for you to anticipate trouble and perhaps avoid it.

'Be prepared!' is as good a motto for managers as it ever was for boy scouts.

CONTINGENCY PLANS

Don't be superstitious about contingency plans and insurance. Preparing for things will not make them happen and you may be able to avoid their happening altogether.

Go through the day-to-day working of your department and list the difficulties and crises that might arise, including the most banal contretemps and the most terrible disasters you can imagine.

Your list might include such things as:

- a serious fire;

- a power failure;
- a strike;
- a surprise visit from the managing director;
- bankruptcy of the suppliers of your department's raw material;
- your right-hand man or woman inherits a fortune or wins the football pools and departs for the Bahamas.

Your list will almost certainly be a long one, but as you work through the worst possible case scenario for each, you will realize that one heading can cover several difficult situations.

For example, your fire scenario will enable you to plan for other disasters like an aircraft hitting your building or a terrorist bomb.

Open a general contingency plan file, containing both general and specific plans, for disasters.

Ask yourself:

- what disaster?
- what is the contingency plan?
- who is responsible for implementing the plan? Who is next in line?
- how long will it take (in stages towards (a) some recovery, (b) semi-recovery and (c) full recovery)?
- what resources will be needed and where are they available?

Keep a copy of your contingency plans in a different location and inform the people there and your senior staff that you have done so.

INVOLVE TO SOLVE

Contingency planning is a good area in which to involve your people and to obtain valuable input on the possible effects of disaster on their workstations and how to minimize them.

You may also find some gaps in your precautionary measures and basic equipment. Don't forget that while you cannot be held responsible for natural disasters, you *are* responsible for things like:

- displaying emergency 'phone numbers where appropriate;
- making sure that fire-fighting equipment is adequate and in working order;
- ensuring that there are enough first aid personnel;
- checking that evacuation procedures are effective and that everyone knows what they are and has practised them.

HAZARDS

Involve your staff in day-to-day safety planning by soliciting their ideas. They are the people who know where the concealed dangers lie and how to avoid them. Not only that, but in addition to making you better able to cope with major disasters and injuries, planning for industrial safety in this way could yield a bonus in the reduction of time lost due to minor accidents.

COPING WITH STRESS

Knowing that contingency plans exist for dealing with serious emergencies and minor 'panics', and that all possible precautions have been taken, will reduce the stress levels of you and your staff.

At the same time, your coaching in disciplines like time management should mean that your staff do not feel overworked, while your efforts to motivate them and make them feel 'happy in their skin' should mean that the atmosphere of your department is relaxed and cheerful.

However, stress is not all bad. Some stress is necessary. You may find that while some people have more stress than they can cope with, others are less stressed than they need to be. It is up to you to see that the correct balance is maintained.

THE POSITIVE AND NEGATIVE EFFECTS

The *positive* effects of stress include: improved alertness, stimulation and reduced reaction times. Stress represents a satisfying challenge if we are able to deal with it.

The *negative* effects of stress include: bad temper, frequent mistakes, lack of flexibility, poor concentration, forgetfulness, tiredness, poor judgement and bad health. This sort of stress is cumulative in that one effect accentuates the others. Avoiding it in both yourself and your staff is vital if you are to run a successful department.

LEARN TO RECOGNIZE STRESS AND ITS CAUSES

Learn first to identify the symptoms of stress, because the stress itself may be caused by factors outside the workplace as well as by job and career worries.

Outside the workplace the main causes of stress are economic and social problems, family worries and apparently minor niggles like poor service or transport difficulties.

The difficulty in recognizing causes is compounded by the fact that in many cases people are unaware of the real reason for their stressed condition and may not even know they *are* stressed.

Look for people who have persistent headaches, who perspire or complain of stomach problems, who tend to over-react, lose concentration or show poor judgement. Such people may also be over-emotional, nervous and irritable. They may complain of sleeping badly. It is possible that their frequent mistakes, excessive drinking or absenteeism will give you a chance to ask them into your office for a chat and an offer of help. Don't be surprised if, after some initial resistance, they begin to treat you as a parent figure. They may just need someone to talk to. If not, their stress may be due to something you can deal with, especially if you have a contingency plan in the form of a list of useful contacts like Alcoholics Anonymous, debt counsellors and so on.

If you have a sympathetic type on your staff you could save yourself some stress by delegating some of the counselling to them. You could also delegate the job of fitness counsellor to an appropriately sporty type with the brief of improving the fitness of the whole department.

By combating stress in this way you may find you are able to make enthusiastic, hard-working employees out of people you have hitherto thought of as 'difficult'.

DIFFICULT PEOPLE

Dealing with 'difficult' people is now seen as one of the most important areas of management, especially for front-line managers whose work brings them into direct contact with relatively large numbers of employees. This is because a few difficult people can cause more problems than the rest of the staff put together, by disrupting production, fomenting discontent, lowering morale and sabotaging managerial initiatives.

Once you have helped the over-stressed individuals – who are not so much difficult people as people with difficulties – you may still be left with some really difficult people ranging from the prickly, awkward or aggressive, to the genuine SOBs.

A LONG-RANGE DIFFICULT PEOPLE POLICY

In the long run, if you are responsible for hiring and firing, you will be able to eliminate many of the really difficult people and most of the SOBs from your department by pursuing a personnel policy of *hire the best, train the rest and get rid of the pest*.

Meanwhile, you have to decide whether your current difficult people are that way by nature or whether there is a reason for their being difficult.

Don't forget that all the difficult people will not necessarily be working for you. You could be working for them.

THE SEVEN RAGES OF MAN

Some difficult people rage outwardly, others inwardly, and among them it is possible to identify seven main personality types. These are:

- *Attackers.* Attackers put their point of view forcibly, often in inappropriate language. They are prone to stand up for their rights to such an extent that they violate the rights of others. They can be hostile, patronizing, contemptuous and are given to blaming other people or external forces for their mistakes. They believe that they are never in the wrong and the trouble is that they may sometimes *be* in the right.

Your action Don't meet aggression with aggression. Speak to the attacker by name and, if they are standing, ask them, quietly but firmly, to sit down. Listen carefully to what they have to say and reply either that you agree and that they are right or that you think that what they say could be right and you will take it under advisement.

- *Egotists.* Egotists also put their views forcibly but some of these big-heads may be eggheads or have genuine specialist knowledge.

Your action Show respect for their knowledge where merited, but don't be intimidated by it. Instead, make use of what they know and if necessary draw them out by asking questions. Compliment and thank them when they provide useful input, but do so in such a way that they realize that while they may be gifted soloists, they are nevertheless subject to the guidance of your conductor's baton.

- *Sneaks.* These people take pot-shots at others, usually from ambush, and take pleasure in dropping their colleagues in the mire. At meetings their main weapon is sarcasm, usually at the expense of those they know will find difficulty in hitting back. They are experts in the use of innuendo.

Your action The line between sneaks and 'sources of information' is often thin. Put an end to innuendo by asking direct questions: 'Has Barry really been stealing from the petty cash? If so, how many times, how much and can you prove it?' Combat malicious tale-telling by telling the sneak that – unless there is a very good reason for not doing so – you intend approaching the person concerned and disclosing not only the accusation but the name of the accuser.

- *Victims.* Like attackers, many victims are specialists in getting their own way. They use submissive behaviour to escape conflict and to avoid guilt feelings: 'It's only little me. What do you expect?'

Your action Identify and help the real victims, the physically weak and the not so bright. Distinguish them from the cringing, hand-wringing, 'ever so 'umble' role-playing Uriah Heaps who can only be changed by finding them an even more effective role. Coach them to be assertive and ask for their suggestions.

- *Negators.* Negators are usually suspicious of those in authority and convinced that their own way of doing things is the only way. They will always oppose you on principle.

Your action Use the negator as a sounding board and a devil's advocate and take the sting out of the negation by actively soliciting it. For example, at group meetings call on the negator as soon as you have outlined your plan: 'Graham, I'm pretty certain you won't be in favour so maybe you could begin by letting us have your objections and perhaps an alternative solution.'

You could get some useful input. After all, if Graham tries to put the block on everything he is bound to be right once in a while. If he is not right, you will usually be able to leave it to his colleagues to demolish his arguments.

- *Super-agreeable people.* Like victims, super-agreeable people may be concealing rage or they may have a compulsive need to be liked, in which case agreeing is their way of trying to get what they want. They are difficult because in their eagerness to please they often over-commit themselves and then turn in a disappointing performance.

Your action Monitor their assignments to make sure they are not overstretched or overworked. Watch for the workplace martyrs who cry out for work and then feel exploited.

- *Unresponsive people.* Often the most difficult of difficult people, unresponsive individuals may be sulking while seething away inside, in which case they are what used to be called 'mute of malice'. On the other hand, they could be a little slow, shy or lacking in education and experience. There's a chance they could even be bored.

Your action Sort out the sulkers and try to find out if they have – or think they have – any genuine reason to be upset. Coach the shy, the slow and the inexperienced, using patience and understanding. Ask open-ended questions that call for more than a one-word answer.

With the others, work on the assumption that you have not yet found the right motivating button to press and try to find out what it is that they really want. If they really want to be left alone, give them the sort of jobs they can do well by themselves, while inviting them to contribute to the team effort from time to time. Reward them if they do a good job and bid them a reluctant farewell if not.

DIFFICULT BOSSES

Many of the techniques which are useful when dealing with difficult employees can be used to cope with difficult bosses. Others cannot. The difference is that your *control* factor when a boss is making your life hell is limited.

It is no use suffering in silence. Ask what is wrong and whether you can help in any way; aim for an adult discussion rather than a confrontation. Maybe you have been doing something to rile the boss, perhaps without even being aware of it.

Do your best, but don't wait for a nervous breakdown or a heart attack. Ask for a transfer or, if the worst comes to the worst, leave.

SOBs AND OTHER IMPOSSIBLE PEOPLE

Do your damnedest to improve difficult members of your staff, but if you come up against bullies, crooks, persistent skivers or people guilty of sexual harassment – get rid!

Give mutineers who go out of their way to flout your authority – as opposed to people whose ideas differ from your own – one chance before putting them overboard in a small boat.

You have been given responsibility – accept it!

THE CONTROL QUOTIENT

Your *control* factor when dealing with difficult situations will be high, provided you have contingency plans which you can implement using the PACA PACA sequence.

As front-line manager your control over stress factors will generally be high and you will be able to work towards a working environment free of negative stress.

When dealing with difficult individuals you will be able to decide whether they are troublesome people or people in trouble and act accordingly. In the end, your control over absolutely impossible people should be absolute.

HOW WILL YOU KNOW YOU HAVE SUCCEEDED?

You will be reassured about your success when your staff take an interest in safety and contingency planning. You will *know* you have succeeded when you meet and overcome your first serious crisis.

Your success in creating a working environment free of negative stress will be apparent when there is a marked decrease in absenteeism and you begin to be aware that you are in charge of a 'happy ship'.

Success in dealing with difficult people is not easy to achieve, but the rewards, when everyone begins to pull their weight, should be equivalent to those you could expect from taking on 5 to 10 per cent more staff.

SUMMARY

- Dealing with difficult situations by planning for them. Making contingency plans for disasters which may never happen.
- Involving staff in contingency planning and why you should consult those people who would be affected.
- Coping with stress. The security of knowing contingency plans exist will remove some stress factors. The symptoms of stress. Delegating stress control.

- Difficult people. Separating the people in difficulty from the genuine SOBs.
- The seven types of difficult people and how to change their attitudes.
- Dealing with SOBs and other 'impossible' people and why the only word which can save your health and your sanity must sometimes be 'goodbye'!

TWENTY

Moving On

Where do you go from here? As a front-line manager you are a member of a profession in which the top people are paid more than a million pounds a year, so it's well worth thinking about your future.

Of course, you may be happy as you are, perhaps because you feel that promotion would be stressful, or perhaps because you are content to give your company value for money and devote the rest of your time and energy to outside interests.

However, if you do want to move on, it's as well to have a plan and to decide where you want to be next year, in five years' time, in ten years' time and later.

Write down your goals in your diary and keep a check on your progress. You may change your route, you could change your destination but, without a map, you stand a very good chance of losing your way.

Not so long ago, most companies provided their new managers with a career 'map' with every stage along the route to the top clearly signposted, but now this is not always the case. Nevertheless, signposted or not, if you are asking 'Where do I go from here?', the first thing to decide is 'Where exactly is here?'.

WHERE IS HERE?

After a year or so in your first front-line manager's job you should have a good idea of how successful you've been, even if your company has no formal assessment programme. Your own regular performance checks will have told you how you and your staff have evolved in each of the important areas of management, and you should have seen a marked improvement in:

- the effectiveness of your leadership;
- the ability of your staff to work as teams;
- the morale and motivation of individual staff members and your staff as a whole;
- your own ability, and that of your senior staff, to delegate and the willingness of individual employees to accept new responsibilities;
- the way you and your staff manage time;
- the communication skills of both you and your staff;
- the use of available technology;
- your department's preparedness to cope with crisis.

At the same time you will have involved your staff in honing their processes so that everyone is doing the best possible job, and whether you run a specific 'quality' programme or not, both you and they will be committed to the ideals of quality, continuous improvement and 'customer' service.

Of course, your fitter, better-motivated and well-coached staff will also have increased production and cut down waste to an impressive extent and your boss could be making appreciative noises.

Mind you, in most cases, while all this has been going on, you will also have had to cope with the daily series of dramas, ranging from stark tragedy to pure farce, which go to make up the workplace 'soap opera' and which are the real stuff of management.

In spite of this, you may be beginning to feel that the job is no longer quite the challenge it was when you first took over, and that your department would run pretty well if you spent a couple of days a week playing golf. You may even have managed to get home in time for dinner once or twice.

This could be the moment to begin thinking in terms of moving up to the next step on the ladder. The trouble is that in some cases your company will have removed the ladder.

HELP! NO CAREER LADDER!

Not so long ago almost all companies had a paternalistic attitude towards their managers and encouraged them to climb to the top of a well-defined career ladder.

Nowadays, although 19 out of 20 companies claim that they regard it as important to develop their high fliers, a good half of them leave their managers to find their own way forward. In fact, even if your current company provides a hierarchic management structure, there is nothing to say that it will continue to do so or indeed any guarantee that the company itself will continue.

The best plan is to behave as though you, and you alone, are responsible for your future progress, while taking every advantage of any career structures and training facilities which may be in place.

PARACHUTES AND PROMOTIONS

Think in terms of 'parachutes' as well as promotion. Times are uncertain and, in an era of change, few people have a secure job for life, or can assume that the perfect boss they are working for at the moment will never be replaced.

Thinking about parachutes or alternative opportunities is a worst possible case scenario exercise. Nothing may happen, but you will feel a lot better if you have a few 'phone numbers in your diary. Besides, there's nothing to say that a parachute can't also be a promotion.

As front-line manager you should form a 'new boy network' of colleagues and plan to be the first person the others call on for help. That way, when you need a favour, it should be – repeat, should be – only a 'phone call away.

THE MULTI-SKILLED MANAGER

In the days when the career ladder was the rule, it was often possible for a manager to get to the top by rising through the grades in a single department like marketing or finance.

Today, top managers need not only the wide-ranging skills we have discussed in previous chapters – like the skills of leadership, team leading and communications – but broad experience in using their skills in different functions, which means working for different departments – or different companies.

Fortunately, as they gain experience and progress in grade, managers become increasingly interchangeable and increasingly mobile, with near-universal managerial skills which call for relatively little adaptation if they change from one industry to another.

Multi-skilling provides the same opportunities and the same security for managers as it does for front-line workers.

THE SPECIALIST MANAGER

Managers who wish to move on, whether on a company ladder or by taking their own route, need to be multi-skilled and mobile, but it can also pay to specialize and even to have a couple of specialities. For example, an experienced manager who is also a computer specialist, or who is proficient in one or more foreign languages, will normally have better promotion prospects than someone who has merely demonstrated competence in day-to-day management.

If you are thinking in terms of promotion, think in terms of your curriculum vitae. Imagine yourself a few years from now in line for your dream job. What sort of c.v. would you like to be able to submit? 'Ten years' loyal service as sales office manager for Bloggs & Co.' might not be enough. Much better if you could say that you had managed several different departments for Bloggs & Co., including perhaps a year in Sienna or Singapore, in addition to which you had been appointed to manage a company-wide quality or motivation initiative. The time you spent white water canoeing and wrestling with tricky problems on the middle management course would look well on your c.v., and having captained the firm's golf or bridge team would do you no harm.

If your dream job calls for selling experience or a diploma in French commercial law, include these items in your forward planning. If you seriously intend to realize your full potential as a manager, the time to begin working on your c.v. is as close to the beginning as possible – not the day you are writing your next job application.

YOUR FUTURE – AND THE FUTURE

When planning your future, don't plan with today in mind, plan for tomorrow. Keep yourself informed about those major trends which will bring many opportunities in their wake.

One such trend is towards internationalism, which will mean that by the year 2000, because of factors like a single European market, most companies' management requirements will be radically different. As *Fortune* magazine put it: 'In a single pivotal decade, Europe will transform itself from a pokey patchwork into a unified, fast-moving market place loaded with opportunities.'

This, together with other moves towards mega-markets, means that the distinction between 'domestic' and 'foreign' markets is no longer important and that, in consequence, the most successful managers will be those who are able to abandon their preoccupation with the home market.

Factors like the increasing concern for the environment will also provide new problems and opportunities for managers, as will the breathtaking speed of change.

Goods are rapidly becoming the same, wherever they are made, and even technological advances are quickly made up and overtaken, which means that service is becoming increasingly important – so much so that it is estimated that by the year 2000 nine out of ten American and European managers will be supplying services rather than goods.

Obviously, experience in improving service as a front-line manager is something which will stand you in good stead in the world market place.

ENGLISH – THE INTERNATIONAL LANGUAGE

On balance, English-speaking managers are favoured by the position of English as the international business language. However, the advantage is not always in favour of the native English speaker. In fact, one very important contract was awarded by a German company to a Finnish firm, rather than its British competitor, simply because the Germans considered they would find it easier to deal in English with English-speaking Finns than with Britons.

British managers in the main are terrible linguists. A British Institute of Management survey revealed that fewer than half of British managers could understand a simple business letter in French, while only 4 per cent could understand the same letter in German, and 5 per cent in Spanish and Italian. As for replying to the letter in the original language, the percentages were halved yet again.

This is a dreadful state of affairs for British business, but one which offers a marvellous window of opportunity to the British front-line manager.

TRAVEL BROADENS THE SCOPE

Visiting foreign countries, even if only as an aware tourist, can provide useful background for potential international managers. Holiday visits will provide both you and your family, if you have one, with language and cross-cultural training, while a vacation course diploma from a foreign university or school of management could increase your chances of a foreign assignment.

Learning a foreign language is only one of the ways in which you can prepare yourself for a job in the international marketplace of the future. You should also take every opportunity to learn about the business culture of other countries. For instance, it could come as a surprise to learn that France, along with such countries as Japan and Mexico, is numbered as a high 'power distance and uncertainty avoidance culture'. This means that 'straight-talking' British, American or Australian managers, with their disregard for protocol and comparative willingness to take risks, will usually need to make adjustments if they are to work in a multi-national environment.

THE STAY-AT-HOME INTERNATIONAL MANAGER

The globe-trotting manager is likely to remain a feature of the international scene but it is unlikely that, a few years from now, all the managers working in the international market will spend their lives in hotels or in the air.

Instead, the trend will almost certainly be towards electronic management backed up by the occasional personal visit, which means that computer literacy will be an increasingly important asset. If you still think a word processor is just a sophisticated typewriter, for example, glance at any current computer magazine to find out how much you *don't* know.

In fact, provided you are willing to regard the whole of your career as a learning experience, everything you do now will stand you in good stead as you move up the ladder. Only the scale and the environment change. The fundamentals of management remain much the same for any managerial post, which is why you will find the Ten Commandments of Management as helpful in the future as you will now.

THE TEN COMMANDMENTS OF MANAGEMENT

- *Remember that management is a people business.* Managers manage people in order to provide goods or services and to make money – for people.
- *Plan to manage.* Planning and decision-making plus flexibility (as instanced by the PACA PACA sequence) are the keys to management success.
- *Involve to solve.* Management means working through other people. Harness their full potential by giving them a stake in the process and if possible the outcome.
- *Accept responsibility; share credit; take blame.* You're the boss and your desk is where the buck stops, whether it's carrying a rose in its mouth or a smoking bomb.
- *Do as you would be done by.* Remember how it feels to work for a really good boss. Make sure your people feel that way.
- *Trust in God but keep your powder dry.* Watch for the rare SOBs whether they are your seniors, your colleagues or

members of your staff. Give people who are out of line at least one chance and usually two, but make sure that on the infrequent occasions when you *do* decide there will be no more 'Mr Nice Guy', the shock waves rattle the building.

- *Help yourself by helping others.* Motivate, inspire and coach your people to realize their full potential – only that way will you materially increase the efficiency and productivity of *your* department.
- *Stroke your folks.* Praise and appreciation, plus the odd bonus, theatre ticket or seat at a boxing match, are the manager's secret weapons. Use them effectively and the rewards will be enormous.
- *Remember that 'Manners makyth managers'.* Be courteous and well mannered to everyone, whatever their position, and coach your staff to follow your example. It not only makes life easier for you and everyone with whom you come in contact but it is the finest way to achieve managerial objectives.
- *Work hard and have fun.* Work should be fun and hard work should enable you to lead a full life outside the workplace. As a manager, you should enjoy both the work and rewards and encourage your people to do the same.

THE CONTROL QUOTIENT

Plenty of the factors which will influence your advancement – especially your ability to plan your c.v. in advance – are within your *control*. All the things which make you a successful front-line manager will stand you in good stead as you move on, so the control quotient is probably much higher than you think.

HOW WILL YOU KNOW YOU HAVE SUCCEEDED?

You will know you have made your head huntable when people start hunting it, and when people both inside and outside your own organization offer you the chance to repeat your success as a front-line manager in jobs with more scope – and more money.

Then, when money becomes a less important consideration

than scope, challenge and job satisfaction, you will be on your way to reaping the major rewards of *moving up to management*.

SUMMARY

- Where do you go from here? The decision to move on is yours but, if you decide to do so, you should have a plan.
- Where is here? How to assess your progress and your potential for advancement.
- How some companies have pulled up their 'career ladders' and why you should behave as though your company is one of them.
- Promotions, parachutes and 'new boy networks', or how to insure your future in a changing and insecure world.
- Planning your c.v. in advance. Why you need to be a mobile, multi-skilled manager with a special skill or two of your own if you are to take full advantage of the mega-markets of AD 2000 and beyond.
- The Ten Commandments of Management.

What to Read and How to Read it

Provided they don't belong to other people, read all management books (including this one) with a highlighter pen handy. It hurts us to say so, but books on management are management tools and the way to get the best from them is to mark the passages that interest you and which you think will be useful.

Read quickly, using the level of speed reading at which you are comfortable, and go back to sections particularly relevant to your needs.

SHORTCUTS

Book reviews in the appropriate journals will help you find books that will interest you and, when talking to fellow-managers, 'Read any good books lately?' is more than a conversational gambit.

Other shortcuts are such books as *Guide to Management Gurus* by Carol Kennedy (Business Books (1991) paperback edn 1993). This is a splendid book which lists 34 of the top management thinkers from Henry Fayol to Tom Peters and Michel Porter. It not only provides the reader with a two- or three-page outline of each writer's theories but also gives a list of their key books.

There's no such thing as a bad guru because all have something to contribute, but seminal authors include: Abraham Maslow of *Hierarchy of Needs* fame; Douglas McGregor, propounder of Theories X and Y; Frederick Herzberg – especially for his couple of pages long 'One More Time: How do you motivate employees?'; Tom Peters, the searcher for excellence;

and Victor Vroom, whose theories on acceptable rewards are as intriguing as his name.

Using this guide will enable you to pin-point those authors whose views are of interest to you and to learn enough about them to hold your own in conversation, while at the same time making it possible to flesh out your knowledge, if you wish to do so.

Similar 'timesavers' include *Writers and Organizations* (Penguin Books (1977) revised edn 1989) and *Organization Theory: Selected Readings* (Penguin Books (1971) revised edn 1990) both by D. S. Pugh and D. J. Hickson, and *Makers of Management* by David and Crainer Clutterbuck (Macmillan, 1990).

CLASSICS

There are many 'classics' which can be read for enjoyment as much as instruction. Those particularly interesting for front-line managers include:

Further up the Organization by Robert Townsend (Coronet Books, 1985). Townsend was director of American Express and chairman of Avis and his book is aimed at everyone 'from CEO to ambitious office boy'. It contains bite-sized chunks of information and iconoclastic opinion from a man who no longer needed to be diplomatic. You may not agree with all he writes but you should not be bored.

Great Leaders by John Adair (Talbot Adair Press, 1989). A fascinating study of the great leaders of history, including 'Margaret Thatcher the Manager' and 'General Montgomery the Motivator'. There's even a piece on Adolf Hitler, revealing him to be a great but flawed leader. A good book to read as background before tackling the huge subject of leadership.

The Complete Time Management System by Christian H. Godefroy and John Clark (Piatkus Books, 1990). This one will have you hoarding seconds and trying to see if you really can save as much time as the authors claim. You may not succeed but you will certainly tighten up the work of your department.

Inside Organizations: 21 ideas for managers by Charles Handy (BBC Books, 1990). Aimed specifically at first-time managers and written to accompany Handy's TV series 'Walk The Talk'. As the subtitle suggests, it's an 'ideas' rather than a 'how-to' book. Mind you, if you find a couple of ideas that you can use in any book you have almost certainly got more than your money's worth and – who knows? – one of them may revolutionize your career and your life.

The Longman Guide to English Usage by Sidney Greenbaum and Janet Whitcut (Longman, 1988). A guide to grammar, spelling and usage which is as clearly written and easy to understand as it is informative and erudite.

The Official High-flier's Handbook by Philip Jenks, Jim Fisk and Robert Barron (Harriman House Publishing, 1993). A marvellous, mickey-taking management book which owes much to Stephen Potter and has the same core of thought-provoking wickedness. A great cure for managerial blues which could also get sluggish synapses snapping again.

Index